You WILL BE FOUND!

How Heavenly Father Knows You & Answers Prayers Individually

How Heavenly Father Knows You & Answers Prayers Individually

Michelle Porcelli

CFI
An imprint of Cedar Fort, Inc.
Springville, Utah

© 2023 Michelle Porcelli
All rights reserved.

No part of this book may be reproduced in any form whatsoever, whether by graphic, visual, electronic, film, microfilm, tape recording, or any other means, without prior written permission of the publisher, except in the case of brief passages embodied in critical reviews and articles.

ISBN 13: 978-1-4621-4496-9

Published by CFI, an imprint of Cedar Fort, Inc.
2373 W. 700 S. Suite 100, Springville, UT 84663
Distributed by Cedar Fort, Inc., www.cedarfort.com

LIBRARY OF CONGRESS CATALOGING-IN-PUBLICATION DATA

Library of Congress Control Number: 2023935147

Cover design by Shawnda Craig
Cover design © 2022 Cedar Fort, Inc.
Edited and typeset by Valene Wood

Printed in the United States of America

10 9 8 7 6 5 4 3 2 1

Printed on acid-free paper

To my family.
Eternity is not long enough.

Contents

Acknowledgments xi

Introduction 1

Chapter One: He Knows Us Individually 3
    Facing Goliath 3

Chapter Two: He Is Mindful of Our Struggles 7
    The Worst of the Best Day 7
    Morning of Be the One 8
    The Following Week 11
    The In-Between—Connecting Current Events to
        Gospel Stories and Principles 12
    Alma Speaking about the "Unspeakables" 13
    What You Already Have 15

Chapter Three: He Offers Redemption 19
    Chasing the Wind 19
    Touch of the Master's Hand 21
    The In-Between—Redemption of Souls 23
    What about the Sinners? 24
    Then Came Noah 25
    Building Your Ark 27

Chapter Four: He Gives Us Spiritual Gifts 31
    The Thing about Abish 31
    The In-Between—We Are Modern-Day Abish 33
    Using Your Spiritual Gifts 35
    Acting on Faith 35
    Don't Knock Me Over 37
    We Can Make a Difference 40

Chapter Five: He Is the Good News **41**
The Good News 41
The In-Between—You Can Control the Narrative 43
Enter Sariah 44
Sariah's Good News 45
Celebrating the Gospel 46
What's in It for You? 48

Chapter Six: He Helps Us Become Self-Reliant **51**
Pop Goes the Weasel 51
Self-Reliance with a Little Bit of Help 54
Forgiveness in All the Right Places 56
What Is Expected from You? 57
But What about Self-Reliance? 58
The In-Between—What Does This Mean to Me? 59
Enter Joseph 60
Spiritual Self-Reliance 62
The Prayer Factor 63

Chapter Seven: He Is Merciful **65**
Meet Popo 65
The In-Between—Second Chances 70
Nineveh 71
Do Our Enemies Deserve a Second Chance? 73
The Lord Is on Your Side 75

Chapter Eight: He Will Guide Us to Safety **77**
You Will Be Found 77
Lost Keys 79
The In-Between—Don't Let Christ's Atonement Be in Vain 80
The Lost Sheep 81
Come unto the Fold 83

Chapter Nine: He Accepts Us as We Are **87**
    Marta the Mighty 87
    The In-Between—Sacrifices 89
    The Widow's Mite 90
    The Bigger Picture 93
    Your Mites 95

Chapter Ten: He Celebrates Diversity **97**
    Cookie Cutters 97
    Uniqueness 99
    Should You Seek to Fit in or Seek to Stand Out? 101
    The In-Between—The Lord Needs Our Diversity 102
    Who Is Your Neighbor? 102
    Different and the Same 104
    Rocking the Boat 105
    The Discomfort Zone 106
    Italians Can Marry Irish, They Make Beautiful Children 109

Chapter Eleven: You Will Be Found! **115**
    No More Missed Chances 115
    Three Miracles So Far, and Counting. 119
    The In-Between—Letting Go of the Self 121
    Enos and Self-Forgiveness 122
    Different, Yet as One 124
    What This Means to Us 125
    The Living Waters 125
    So, What Happened? 126
    God Knows You and Answers Prayers Individually 126

About the Author **129**

Acknowledgments

THANKS TO MY FAMILY WHO HAVE SUPPORTED ALL MY CRAZY ADVENtures and ideas. Some ideas have worked, some not, and some have been miraculous game changers in our lives. I stand by my philosophy: "Fall 99 times, get up 100."

Thanks to those who know my entrepreneurial mind and like me anyway. It seems I need to have thousands of brain windows open to just feel sane. I have found my tribe of those who understand my drive and encourage me along the path. When in doubt, "step on the gas." We truly create our own limits.

Thanks to all those before me who have paved the way making it cool to talk about Jesus. He deserves to be celebrated with every breath we take.

Finally, thanks to my Father in Heaven who I have felt influence my thoughts and ideas. You have always been there, even when I felt forgotten. All I needed to do was reach out to find your calming spirit and Father's blessing to help spread light and love to the world.

Introduction

....

WITH OVER SEVEN BILLION PEOPLE ALIVE ON EARTH TODAY, IT IS normal to wonder if God actually knows us individually, and if that is even possible. I think of my parents who had six children. How could they love each one of us equally even though our needs were so different? Or, did they instead hold a higher love in order to match our current and individual needs?

When I was very young, my father had a heart attack and I was left home alone, a lot. Did my mother love me less because she left me to fend for myself? No. She needed to attend to my father's needs and trusted I would keep the door locked and behave appropriately. She still showed love to me in different ways. I remember her teaching me how to make my first batch of Kraft macaroni and cheese. I now consider myself an expert and this miracle invention was my dinner for many weeks. The point is, love can be shown in different ways and according to our current situations.

As an elementary school counselor, I serve over a thousand children each year, all with different struggles. When they enter my office, they think I remember every detail of our prior conversations, even if we hadn't spoken in a very long time. They all feel like I know them individually. Although I do often forget details, I do the best I can to make them feel important and worthwhile when they are with me. When I think about all my students and their personal stories I try to keep sorted out in my head, I can only imagine all the details Heavenly Father has to keep straight. However, He does this perfectly.

God is our eternal Father and knew each of us before our individual earth life. I believe He was there to send us off on our journey, knowing the trial and triumphs we would experience and could choose to learn from. It is common for people to blame God when things go wrong and then celebrate Him when things go right. However, it is not God's job to make sure our lives our smooth. It is His job to give us learning opportunities so that we may prove ourselves worthy to return to Him. It is our job to get to know Him, live by the commandments, and do our best to be good humans.

The purpose of this book is to give you insights on how God knows you individually and answers our prayers according to His desire for our lives. We may not always get the answers we want, but we will get the learning opportunities we can use to strengthen our eternal bonds. We will explore experiences of those living in different cultures and situations, along with exploring scriptural accounts of when people needed to turn and listen to God. His work is in the details.

Many stories I have included are based on true accounts but have been fictionalized to protect those involved. I have received permission for each personal story shared. However, any likeness to someone you know is unintentional and likely a coincidence. If they want you to know the story is specifically about them, they will let you know.

Chapters 2–11 contain an "In-Between" section to help the reader relate current events to gospel principles, stories in the Book of Mormon, the Bible, and relate to words of the prophets. This is to help the reader understand how God is omnipresent and in the details of our everyday lives. He existed in the past, is in our present, and will be in our future.

Most important, my hope is that this book strengthens testimonies and stands as a witness that you are not forgotten. These stories testify of God and His son, Jesus Christ. They stand as a proclamation to the wandering; you will be found!

Chapter One

He Knows Us Individually

....

Facing Goliath

THE CRACKLING CEMENT ON THE DRIVEWAY MARKED THE PATHWAY leading into the dusty garage. The smell of gasoline leaking from our old convertible permeated the air, my heart rate continued to increase, and I didn't know if I could do it. Would I be able to take on my own challenge? The jaunts and cheers from the onlookers didn't help. They encouraged me to continue my quest and I could see their cell phones rising into the air in hopes of filming a good TikTok- or YouTube-worthy scene from our latest escapade. This event would likely get them many views. I rolled my eyes at them and made a face as I said, "Watch this!"

Not long before this moment, my child had screamed in fear upon seeing the shiny widowed spider in our garage. Her chore was to clean out the convertible, remove all the trash and put it into the bin. Kids will generally find any excuse they can to get out of something they don't want to do, and I knew this time was no exception. "Emily, you're not getting out of it. I don't care if there are a million black widows crawling all over the seat," I sternly responded to her shriek. I always did have a "Marie Barone" way of making a bad situation worse.

Her tears trailed down her rosy cheeks and dripped onto the pavement. My heart softened and I calmed her heart as I responded, "I'll take care of it. Where is it?" My other daughters, Taylor and Ashley, giggled as they pointed to the shelf just above the driver's side of our cute vehicle, which was ironically branded a Mitsubishi Eclipse Spyder. I knew I couldn't let Emily down this time. "We named her Goliath," Taylor announced. "So, does that make me David?" I smirked. Their imaginations were running wild, and they couldn't wait to see my reaction when I saw her oversized body and red hourglass belly.

I reached up to the high shelf while holding crinkly toilet paper in my hand. Quilted Northern 2-ply would be my only defense against the dark culprit. "Hold on a minute," I announced as I quickly pulled my hand back down. "Why don't we all do something first?" I suggested. "What Mom, are you chickening out?" Ashley taunted. Taylor was still filming and awaiting my next move.

"I think we all need to say a prayer first," I requested with hopeful anticipation they would all agree. With grunts, groans, and a few eye rolls, the four of us rallied into a circle and Taylor turned off her phone. Ashley offered the prayer that we could find the spider, not kill it, and we would still all be okay. "Not kill it? Really, Ashley?" Emily questioned, obviously upset. I was definitely in a pickle. How was I going to get the black widow out of the garage without killing it?

Did I have faith in the previous prayer? This led to the girls discussing—no—more like arguing about how we needed to have faith in God. They each touted what faith looked like to each of them. Emily said that God would help us kill the spider. Ashley argued God would help us only if we did *not* kill the spider. So, who was right? Taylor didn't even know if God would help us at all and the spider would likely get away and the car still wouldn't be cleaned.

I went inside the house and grabbed a pickle jar. Taylor cried, "Don't dump out my pickles," as I put the contents into another

CHAPTER ONE: HE KNOWS US INDIVIDUALLY

container. I approached the shelf as I slowly walked over to the convertible, climbed in, and used the driver's seat as a height booster. I saw some quick movements and then she appeared in all her glory. Just above me was a huge, smooth, black, red bellied, dominant spider. I reached up, ready to take quick and unwavering action. Her dark glistening eyes seemed to be staring right at me. She was saying, "If you don't kill me, I'm going to bite you. You know that, right?" My emotions got the better of me and I quickly reached down and took off my shoe. Without uttering a word to my girls, I raised the shoe high above my head and made a swift smacking motion. Bam! I bravely knew I had smashed that wicked spider.

I lifted up the shoe slightly above the shelf, expecting to see the spider remains on the bottom, but there was nothing there. I looked onto the shelf to see where the spider was, again nothing. The spider was gone. We panicked wondering if the spider was on one of us. We all screamed as I jumped down from the car and we ran out of the garage. Where had the spider scurried off to? Everyone began lifting up their feet and looking around while patting all over their bodies to make sure she wasn't hiding anywhere close.

Ashley was mad I tried to kill it. Emily was mad I didn't kill it. Taylor was mad she didn't get a very good video out of the entire fiasco.

I felt like I had failed my girls and taught them the opposite of faith. How could they each have a different expectation from God in that situation? How could they each get their way if their prayers were the opposite of each other?

I learned how unique each human really is and also how our expectations of God will also be unique according to each person's perspective. Our relationship with Heavenly Father is truly individualized according to our own needs and desires. It is up to us to create that relationship with Him and understand the meaning of our experiences.

We never did find that dang spider. We continue to wonder why she was allowed to get away. I know Heavenly Father answered all of our expectations in a very unique way. Until we learn to reach up in faith, trusting the Lord will also reach back, we will remain stuck and confused just like when I asked, "Where did it go?" We need to stick to His plan for it is a plan of happiness. We will have many Goliaths, or black widows, in our lives, but we also have the knowledge and gifts to face these trials and become faithful and brave like David.

I know black widows are nothing in comparison to the hardships we face in our lives. However, I do know that small obstacles can lead to large roadblocks. I also know that small miracles can lead to vast and abiding faith. I have had many of my own David versus Goliath moments that I now share with you.

I hope you will enjoy these fictional and non-fictional stories, although some do not have an expected ending. I pray you will know Heavenly Father has given each of us the capacity to reach out to Him, with faith, and the ability to taste heaven. He answers our prayers individually, not according to our desires. With His infinite wisdom He understands which experiences will be the most magnificent test of our faith and teach us humility. He wants us to succeed as we desire to obtain the kingdom of heaven. It is up to us to trust the journey and decide what to learn from, what to embrace, what to let go of, and what to share with our fellow man. I have chosen to share some experiences I hold dear to my heart and am grateful for this opportunity to hopefully make your day a little bit brighter, testimony a little bit stronger, and leave your heart full of the Spirit of Christ.

I dedicate these stories of triumph, guilt, happiness, disappointment, sorrow, love, and growth to my family. Through all our bumps and bruises, even chasing spiders, we have triumphed in our experiences by trusting in the Lord. We have faced our personal Goliaths, and come out of darkness and into the light, hand in hand together.

Chapter Two

He Is Mindful of Our Struggles

The Worst of the Best Day

The sea of faces swiftly rushed by me, creating a blur, and I couldn't find him. I couldn't find the one; the one who was saved that miraculous day. I walked down the school hallway as students quickly brushed past me, some bumping shoulders in the middle path as others hugged the wall. Was he here today? He had to be.

He was the reason I stayed at the school instead of going out to lunch with the rest of my team. He was the reason I fought so hard to create the most controversial program at school: Be the One. The program where we got real about emotions, life, relationships, and beliefs. This special day students were able to make friends outside of cliques, social norms, and expectations.

I first met Cameron during his sophomore year. He would sit slumped over in the chair, trying to act cool and collected. His mom had previously contacted me revealing he had lost his sister the year before and she was worried she was going to lose him too. We worked on building a relationship of trust and then one day Cameron confided in me that he had created a path to end his own life.

As a school counselor, I wish I could encourage faith in students, but with religious limitations, we use the word "hope." I knew Cameron felt no hope. However, I challenged him to come to school the next day for *Be the One*. This was a workshop that gave students an opportunity to connect and interact in a safe and structured environment with a lot of adult support. The program was new, and many counselors were against it because it took so much effort and lacked follow-up. However, I knew these students needed something to show them they matter, and it was worth the risk to me.

After describing the workshop to him, he said, "No way. Tomorrow is my birthday and I'm getting my license." This meant he would have access to the family car. I later found out he had previously planned to use this same car as a path to his doom. "Also, it sounds too touchy feely to me. It's not my type of thing." My heart ached as I knew he was about to choose out of one more thing that could be an opportunity for him to find self-worth and inspiration for his future.

I begged him to come to school just one more day, one more chance at life, one more chance at hope. I told him how the workshop offered opportunities to belong to a makeshift "school family group" where he could make new friends and feel included. He sat hunched over in his chair looking unamused. I couldn't believe my ears when he looked up and said, "Okay, only because you asked me to. I don't think I'll like it, but I'll come." Was it really that easy? Cameron had no hope in himself, and he was just waiting for someone else to have hope for him. I chose his adult leader very carefully and placed him in a group that included some of the kindest kids from our school. I wanted to set him up for success.

Morning of Be the One

What I am about to tell you will likely not be believed by those who never believe. However, for those who always believe or even have a

CHAPTER TWO: HE IS MINDFUL OF OUR STRUGGLES

desire to believe, they have learned how to recognize the miracles in everyday occurrences.

It was a brisk spring morning and the bell was just about to ring signaling that first period was over. Cameron had just earned his driver's license and came straight to school only to tell me he wasn't attending the rest of the day nor attending *Be the One*. I was in the school gym setting up for the program and students were arriving and taking their seats excited to see the fun activities we had planned.

Cameron had parked the family car in the school parking lot and told me he was going to take it joy riding instead of coming to school. I was surprised that he was okay confessing all of this to me and still expecting me to do nothing about it. Then, my prevention training kicked in. No, it was the Holy Ghost. The Holy Ghost reminded me to trust my training and to see the words that were not spoken.

I knew what Cameron was going to do with that car. He had mentioned canyons and cliffs before and his joy ride wasn't going to end well. Unbeknownst to staff and students, I am constantly praying inside my heart. I am always seeking Heavenly Father's guidance in what to say, do, and teach. "Cameron, you committed to coming today and you need to keep your word," I pleaded with him.

Upon hearing this, he didn't know if I was being manipulative or merely reminding him of our prior conversation when he told me he would attend that activity. His eyes shifted downward, looking at the ground as if in deep thought. He looked up at me, making quick eye contact and then quickly looked down at his keys which he had previously plopped onto my desk. As he reached for the keys, I said, "Don't do it."

Then he rebelliously grabbed the keys, turned, and ran out my door, bolting out of the counseling office. He knew I would follow him. He knew I had to. He knew "the one" mattered to me. I called administrators for help as I ran down the school hallway chasing after him. But he was too fast. Once he had passed the auditorium doors at the other end of the building, I was in a panic. He was a good 50 yards ahead of me as he crashed his body through the double doors opening to the south parking lot. He reached his car before anyone else could even come through the exit.

My heart was sinking and my breathing was getting heavier. This couldn't be happening. I silently prayed for a miracle. Was God listening? Does God save the one? What happened next grew faith in all those who chose to participate. By this time, Cameron was inside his car. With the key in the ignition, he was desperately pumping gas to the engine. But it wouldn't start. He tried anxiously to get that engine to turn over, but the reliable car that mom said never had problems before, nor had problems since, wouldn't start.

Everything then seemed to roll by in slow motion, like we were in a movie, as we were approaching the vehicle. As I ran to the driver's side of the car, I could see Cameron sliding out of his seat, opening the door and standing up to greet me. As I arrived at his side, he reached up his hands and collapsed into my arms, nearly knocking me over. He was now in tears, and so was I, as we wept together. He sobbed, "I don't really want to die."

The other administrators quickly came over and wrapped their arms around the both of us. Right in the middle of that school parking lot we had what some may call a "group hug." I call it a miracle. I call it hope. I call it the Holy Ghost working overtime.

This day we all knew the one was saved. It wasn't the program or activities we took months to plan that saved Cameron. It was the inspiration that committed him to come to school, even if he only intended to stay for a moment, because his school counselor asked him to. It was the relationship of trust created between a student and an adult that opened the door to inspiration. Although over one-hundred fifty students were awaiting the days event in the gym, he was the one that mattered that needed us most that morning. We knew the other adult leaders kept the other students safe while a few could attend to a triaged need. I testify it was the Holy Ghost that got him into my office that morning. The Holy Ghost gave him courage to tell me the truth knowing how I would respond.

CHAPTER TWO: HE IS MINDFUL OF OUR STRUGGLES

The Following Week

Through the swarm of faces rushing to class before the bell rings, I finally saw him. I saw the one. I walk down the hall and give him a high five. He then said, "But Mrs. Porcelli, we're supposed to greet each other like this." Cameron folds his fingers to make an "I love you" symbol. "Oh, you are right. I forgot the students decided to greet each other this way all week." Although I couldn't say it out loud, I did love all these students, even the ones I didn't know well.

Sometimes people wonder if they are in the right profession. It took me growing into my forties to find my tribe, meaning the people who have my same passions and energy. I found I belong in the schools working as a counselor. I witness God moments and miracles every day. If we take time and make space for these moments, we see God all around us. We can see the Savior's hand in everyday life. This faith in Christ can give us courage to face our lives and to give charity, our time and efforts, to others along the path.

Moroni 10:20
Wherefore, there must be faith; and if there must be faith there must also be hope; and if there must be hope there must also be charity.

God does not grant to all of us our desires at the same time. Cameron wanted the car to start; I was praying it wouldn't start. Which one of us does God love best and will grant our prayer over the other? He doesn't love either one "best," but rather answers our prayers individually. Cameron admitted he didn't really want the car to start. He did, however, want hope. God granted his unspoken prayer and gave him hope.

As the many years have passed, I have not had much contact with my former student. His mother updated me and said he is doing well and has created an amazing future for himself. I know there will continue to be roadblocks in his life just as there are roadblocks in everyone's life. But on that day years ago, we all know we witnessed something no one has been able to explain since. Maybe we aren't supposed to explain it, but rather just feel it. We felt the Spirit in our lives.

The In-Between— Connecting Current Events to Gospel Stories and Principles

Whenever we have a day where we feel stressed, confused, or even forgotten, we can know that God lives and loves us. He even loves a young man enough to interfere with the ignition of his car.

How does the story of Cameron relate to the gospel of Jesus Christ? The Church of Jesus Christ of Latter-day Saints teaches that we believe in repentance and forgiveness. We believe that children, siblings, friends, neighbors, and even co-workers are capable of redemption. We believe in second chances.

Although we likely know the doctrine of repentance and forgiveness, we seem to continually hold grudges, often choosing to get out of relationships, claiming we are standing on higher ground than those who trespass against us. Repentance is hard. Forgiveness is just as difficult. Neither were meant to be easy.

However, we have examples of prophets, apostles, and everyday people who have overcome the natural man. They have learned how to repent and have also learned how to forgive. It does take practice and can get easier over time. Forgiveness is not so much about the other person repenting or telling us they are sorry, but more about our own state of the heart. Forgiveness doesn't mean what the other person did is okay, but instead means that what happened no longer has control over our spiritual being. We have chosen to set our heart, mind, and soul free from the weighty chains of grudge holding. We have surrendered to God.

One story from the Book of Mormon that teaches about a son's repentance and a father's forgiveness is the story of Alma and Alma the Younger. Alma's forgiveness didn't excuse his son's actions, but instead he pled to our Heavenly Father for God's intervention and asked for a miracle.

CHAPTER TWO: HE IS MINDFUL OF OUR STRUGGLES

Alma Speaking about the "Unspeakables"

Alma 32:21
And now as I said concerning faith—faith is not to have a perfect knowledge of things; therefore if ye have faith ye hope for things which are not seen, which are true.

Whenever I think of Alma, I think of a parent who loves his child with all his heart, even when the child was acting like a brat, ignoring his righteous upbringing, and instead causing heartache all over the town. Yes, I indeed just called Alma the Younger a brat, meaning his behavior before the mighty miracle happened. I'm sure many of you can relate to this opinion. Some children are given the best parents, yet these same children sometimes turn out to be the meanest bullies, the roaring rebellious, and surprise everyone when they turn their backs on God. Even church leaders themselves have children who have turned their hearts away from the gospel. How can this be? Did the parents do something wrong? What should they do differently?

As we read about the example of Alma, we learn he prays for God to intervene with his son, Alma the Younger. His prayer was eventually answered. While Young Alma was sinning and denying the gospel, an angel appeared to him and his sidekicks, the Sons of Mosiah. The angel's words testified of God and told Alma the Younger his father had been praying for his heart to turn toward God. The angel was an answer to Alma's prayer. The message was so powerful, Young Alma was astonished and left paralyzed. He and the Sons of Mosiah had just witnessed a father's prayer being answered. They had just witnessed a miracle. Alma the Younger couldn't speak or move his arms and legs so the Sons of Mosiah took him to his father. Alma didn't know if his son was ever going to recover or be able to speak again. However, Alma had more faith in God than he did in man and knew whatever was going to happen, God was in control.

When I was chasing Cameron down the school hallway, I didn't know how things were going to evolve. I had to put my trust in myself and co-workers and ultimately put trust in God. I knew God would take care of the situation after we had done all we could do. My main duty was to prepare my heart for the miracle.

Parents often want miracles for their children who have had difficulties in life ranging from rejection, having no friends to play with on the school playground, to sorrow from not making the basketball team. Others pray mightily their child will get the college scholarship, while others pray for children to find a worthy mate to be sealed to in the temple. All of our needs are so different, and God answers us each differently.

Some parents may want a very different type of miracle and pray for their child who has fallen away from the gospel. Alma was this type of parent. His son, Alma the Younger, already had popularity, friends, and followers. He used this power to direct many down the path of darkness into a life of sin. He fit in just fine as he was a leader among the wicked. Alma didn't care about his son fitting in, making the team, or other desire we may relate to. I'm not saying current parenting issues and desires don't have merit. But I believe there is something deeper we also could be striving for regarding our children. I call this the "unspeakables" because many parents are embarrassed if their children don't turn out the way the religious culture has deemed acceptable. Because of this, they often don't reach out for help nor reveal struggles their children or family may be experiencing.

I know of many parents who are often working overtime praying for the spiritual or mental ills we see so many suffering from today. Hearts are breaking and some parents are feeling powerless and forgotten. But our God is a God of hope. He has given us a guidebook to take us on this path of life. The scriptures are full of examples of other parents who simply love their children and seek God's guidance to heal the broken heart and mend the aching mind.

After diligently fasting and praying for two days and two nights, Alma the Elder then witnessed another miracle. Young Alma awoke, got up from his bed, and was able to move and speak to the people. I can only imagine what elder Alma must have felt like when he heard his son say, "I have repented of my sins, and the Lord has forgiven me." Young Alma had been repenting to the Lord during the entire time he was paralyzed and while Alma had fasted and prayed. Young Alma had been going through his own Gethsemane. He had to recognize his sins and understand how his actions had affected all the people he taught false doctrine to. He also had to bear the pain, knowing the people he had harmed physically and emotionally. I can only imagine how difficult, yet wondrous those days with the Lord must have been.

Alma the Younger was a changed man and bore testimony to the people that although he once rejected Christ, he knew that Jesus was the Son of God and Redeemer of the World.[1]

Having some of my own children and relatives turn away from the gospel has been one of the hardest things I have experienced. I often pray for them to have an experience like Alma the Younger, but every time I see these children I think, "Oh, so you're still okay? Hmmm. I thought you would have been 'zapped' by now." Yes, funny but not funny. I am not praying for their doom, but rather I am praying for their change of heart. It has been hard to have faith that God is in control, but it is also freeing to know that the Savior has already carried this burden and that one day every knee shall bow and every tongue confess that Jesus is the Christ (Mosiah 27:31; Philippians 2:10–11). This will be the most beautiful day. Through my experiences I have learned that each child is having their own journey in life. As parents our role is to teach them, guide them, and love them fiercely, having faith God will make up for the rest.

What You Already Have

It was springtime and we could hear the birds chirping outside the window during our afternoon Relief Society lesson. We were discussing "How to Help Children Who Left the Gospel" and the room was quite somber among these humble parents who loved their children. There were many tears shed as some shared their experiences of sorrow knowing their children are not on the covenant path. Although I still have great sorrow and my heart often hurts for those who have left the gospel, I believe we can choose to look at life with a brightness of hope. I felt inspired to say something regarding children who choose differently than parents had hoped: "We should not mourn the child we lost, but instead celebrate the child we have." All of God's children were born good. We all have good qualities and I think those

---

1. "The Conversion of Alma the Younger," *Liahona,* May 1988, churchofjesuschrist.org.

attributes often get overshadowed when we focus on one sin or one ideation that may differ from our own. I discussed with one mom that when we mourn it is because we know what they are missing out on. But I firmly believe God will make up the difference when they turn their heart towards Christ. The "when" is in God's timing.

If we focus on what we have lost, we will miss out on what we have. Our children can still offer love, vibrancy, accomplishments, and be a contributing member to society and contribute in our families. As a counselor I will often have parents come to my office and want me to correct their child's behavior. They will often complain how sassy or lazy their children are at home. Some parents may leave my office unsatisfied that I don't have a magic wand I can wave in order to control the choices of others. However, I assure all of them that most children turn out just fine in the long run. Some children may be taking the scenic route, some are taking the erupting volcano route, and others are still floating on the ocean blowing in the wind. But, if we focus on the relationship we have with them now, they will feel of our intense love and the hearts of the children will indeed turn to their fathers (3 Nephi 25:6). This parent/child bond will become stronger than anything Satan can throw at you.

I am not blinded to reality and know that some children will choose to put unhealthy things into their bodies and their minds. They may use their agency to make some very unfortunate decisions. This could include involvement in drugs, breaking the law, moral indiscretion, and even denying the existence of God. However, I have ultimate hope that those children who have been sealed to us will realize those bonds of eternal covenants are much stronger than anything the adversary will throw our way. We can seek to release his clenching grip and reclaim our children, as an eternal family, and to return to the Father someday.

Proverbs 22:6
Train up a child in the way he should go: and when he is old he will not depart from it.

Most parents I know deserve a break from the guilty conscious Satan wants us to hold onto that could ultimately lead to you doubting our own faith. Whether you are a parent, aunt, uncle, grandparent,

CHAPTER TWO: HE IS MINDFUL OF OUR STRUGGLES

teacher, neighbor, or friend, you likely have taught these children true and correct principals in some fashion somewhere along their path. You have been an example of forgiveness, hope, and charity. Be good to yourself. God wants you to know He's got this.

God answered my prayers with my former student. God answered Alma's prayers for his son. Each prayer expressed hope for another soul to be saved. I testify and believe God is in the business of saving souls.

Chapter Three

He Offers Redemption

....

Chasing the Wind

Her short, chubby legs were running as fast as they could, but could they get there in time? The cool wind was blowing against her face, and she could feel the bumpy cold ground beneath her feet as her breathing grew heavier. "Don't trip, don't trip," she commanded herself over and over. She could see the shadow of the plane approaching overhead, undoubtedly headed for an unfortunate end. The engine was sputtering, "dreewip, dreewip," the sound signaling defeat. But she was determined and wanted to use all her strength to make her father proud. She knew she had to get there in time to prevent the crash . . .

"Run, Michelle, run!" her father shouted, the sound echoing throughout her ears. Then, it happened. One last gust of wind was all it took, and the plane made one last swoop out of her reach and boomed nose first into the dead yellow ground of the large practice field. The model airplane not only crashed but had broken into pieces all while the engine was still running. Michelle knew the disappointment in her father's face would be unbearable as she fell to the ground and sobbed into her scrunched up arms which were now tightly folded across her chest. Why didn't Heavenly Father help her run faster knowing how important this was to her? Isn't He the God of miracles? Didn't He love her enough to not let her fail?

While these sorrowful thoughts raced through her head, she felt a warm hand on her back gently offering support to her wailing of tears. Her father had now knelt down beside her as she peered up and looked into his turquoise blue eyes. He tried to console, "Oh Michelle. It's okay. Don't you know? Now I can build a new one!" Michelle was surprised by his calm reaction and knew that her father's heart was softened by the Spirit. He had every right to be upset, but he didn't show any resemblance to anger. Instead, he chose to strengthen a relationship with his daughter rather than anguish over his broken plane.

Heavenly Father appears at the most important of times. It was important to save the plane, but it was more important to save a relationship between a father and his daughter. That earthly father was inspired to say those tender words offering forgiveness and hope.

I'm sure you have guessed by now that this little girl was me. Although this happened decades ago, the emotions and feelings are still very raw. I loved practicing with my dad. It was our time to celebrate all his hard work and hours he spent in the basement cutting, sanding, gluing, and painting wood. He would take days upon days traveling to hobby stories to find the right size engines to match those gliders. Those memories will be held onto forever. I will always cherish chasing those planes and the opportunity I had to learn forgiveness, redemption, and how to hold onto hope.

CHAPTER THREE: HE OFFERS REDEMPTION

Touch of the Master's Hand

I wish you could have known my dad. His health declined as the years passed, and his spine began to curve, hunching his once able body into an arc shape appearance. You see, in his last years, Dad had Parkinson's disease. He shuffled when he walked and whispered when he talked, but his spiritual stature grew stronger as he continued to age. I remember the first time he had completely read the Book of Mormon; it was the year before his death when was eighty-seven years old. Mom claims that he didn't actually read it out loud because of his speech issue. She shared with me how she would read the scriptures out loud to him while he listened intently. At times they would listen to the scriptures on tape and with each chapter completed, they colored in the chart claiming their progress toward their goal. They often read books out of order but finished their goal in December of 2018 with a picture to document and commemorate the event.

As the youngest in the family, my parents were nearly forty when I was born and, to me, always seemed to act so old. They were

homebodies and not very active physically as they approached their senior years. Dad had settled into the life of an accountant and numbers replaced adventures. It wasn't until after Dad passed that I reminisced and reawakened all the memories of when he was vibrant and excited about life.

Wonderfully, Dad was a pilot in the United States Air Force. He loved planes. He loved them so much that after the service he decided to become a hobbyist and build his own model planes. He would compete in air shows around the state and often win. Sometimes he would build gliders without an engine, and other times he would build larger planes. It was a common practice to go for drives throughout Salt Lake City and stop by every hobby store to find the right size engine, wheels, or other piece to match the magnificence of his creations. His basement was soon full of kits, plywood, glue, and a tiny black and white TV he used to keep him company while the master was at work.

I loved watching him carefully carve out the shapes of the wings or tail and then attach all the pieces to create the aircraft. But the most exciting part was when he would bring out his remote control and want to practice. This meant I would be able to help him master the movements and also see how fast the plane could go. Mom would often request I go with him to the practice field just west of Mount Jordan Middle School. Dad thought I was there to catch the planes in case the wind gushed up and caught one of the wings by surprise. However, before leaving to the field, Mom would pull me aside whispering that my "real" main job was to make sure Dad made it home on time for dinner. My top-secret mission was always a challenge to complete, and we often didn't make it home before 6 p.m. when the dinner bell would ring. We would often be much later than hoped, but Mom never seemed overly upset about it.

Throughout life, Dad would get frustrated with me about certain things, but he was never upset with me over his planes. He was always elated when he would practice, as if he was in his prime element, and he was hopeful even when a plane crashed. I think he enjoyed the process of making and repairing planes as much as he enjoyed the flying of them. I learned a valuable lesson that fretful day when I couldn't reach the plane in time and it smashed to the ground. My dad wasn't trying to teach me to run faster than the wind. Rather, he was teaching me resilience, that broken things can be repaired, and sometimes we get to start over with creating new pieces to the puzzle. Whether that puzzle is a model airplane or a symbol of broken experiences in life, when we trust in the Lord, old things become new, and that which was broken becomes whole again (2 Corinthians 5:17).

The In-Between — Redemption of Souls

AMONG THE MANY TITLES USED TO DESCRIBE THE SAVIOR, THE TITLE of Redeemer brings hope to the wandering. To redeem means to pay off a debt or meet an obligation. Redeem can also mean to rescue or set free. If someone commits a mistake but then later corrects it or makes amends, we say he has redeemed himself.[1]

We've all been there, feeling guilty for having sinned against God or letting Him down when knowing the Savior suffered for our sins in the Garden of Gethsemane. No one knows how long Christ was in that garden, but it was long enough to feel every spiritual, emotional, and physical terror that would have destroyed the natural man. However, Christ knew He had God on His side, this was part of the greater plan, and He had knowledge of the universe, and thus Gethsemane did not destroy Him. Rather, He is a survivor and can understand every little pain, sorrow, or regret we may ever experience. He redeemed us. His sacrifice means we have the ability to repent, make amends, and repair or start over. This redemption is not just about atonement and the ability we have to repent, but it is also about the resurrection and the opportunity we have to live.

This chance for redemption offers the idea that, rather than focusing on the crashes, instead focusing on the opportunities to rebuild and restore. We can only learn from the past and look forward to the future, but we must choose to live in the present. My dad's broken planes may be unrepairable, but the relationship that was strengthened will survive beyond the veil and into the eternities. Redemption is about having an eternal perspective and not being stuck in the past.

---

1. D. Todd Christofferson, "Redemption," *Ensign*, May 2013, 109–112.

What about the Sinners?

As much as we don't want to, we all will make mistakes. We will sin. We will repent. We will sin again. That is the reality as long as we are living in human bodies. It is also part of the plan to learn from experiences and then do better by accessing the Atonement and seeking for the Spirit to accompany our journey in life.

> ### *Doctrine and Covenants 58:43*
> *By this ye may know if a man repenteth of his sins—behold, he will confess them and forsake them.*

God has required us to be accountable for our lives and allows us to make certain choices. The redemption from our own sins is conditional. Redemption is conditioned on us confessing and then abandoning sin. As we read in Doctrine and Covenants 58:43, this means turning to a godly life, or in other words, *redemption is conditioned on repentance.*

It is not easy to repent when someone feels hopeless or like God has abandoned them. Satan's plan is for you to feel like there is no redemption and that God has forgotten and doesn't care about you. He wants you to feel like I first did when the model plane crashed; like I had let down my father and there was no repair. However, I learned my earthly father loves me and forgives the "crashes." Your Father in Heaven loves you so much He allowed His begotten son to be sacrificed on your behalf. Do you understand the significance of that?

Think of someone you love with all your heart, might, mind, and soul. Think of your relationship with them and how they have mattered to you during this earth life. Now, ponder on how you would feel if you were to lose them. Think of what it would be like to know their life was not only sacrificed, but was tortured. (Is that too strong of a word? It is certainly the truth of what happened to the Savior physically, emotionally, and spiritually.)

Think of having your special person being offered up and then willingly tortured for someone else that would sin, sin again, and then these same people harass them, rebel, and even deny their existence. Could you do that? Could you sacrifice this person you love so much for a group of people who would later mock the situation as something contrite, made up, and of no consequence?

This may sound dramatic, but there is nothing simple about the sacrifice Heavenly Father and His son, Jesus Christ, made for you. Christ was not only born, but also died so that others may live, not in ignorance, but live with the full light of the gospel and hope of redemption. Don't waste the redemption.

But the awesome thing about God is that He is all about repentance and do-overs, as long as we don't continue to sit in the same situation using the Atonement as an excuse to keep sinning.

The good news is . . . it is not too late for God to work wonders through you. There are numerous examples in the scriptures that talk about ordinary people doing extraordinary things.

Genesis 6:5–8
And God saw that the wickedness of man was great in the earth, and that every imagination of the thoughts of his heart was only evil continually.

And it repented the Lord that he had made man on the earth, and it grieved him at his heart.

And the Lord said, I will destroy man whom I have created from the face of the earth; both man, and beast, and the creeping thing, and the fowls of the air; for it repenteth me that I have made them.

But Noah found grace in the eyes of the Lord.

Then Came Noah

One of the greatest stories of redemption in the Old Testament is the story of Noah. The people were wicked and had fallen away from the commandments of God. God warned of a coming judgment that was going to be a worldwide punishment.

God told Noah to build an ark. Can you imagine what the neighbors must have thought? It certainly wasn't socially acceptable to follow God and Noah must have appeared to have a few loose screws. I'm sure even those who considered themselves good people were among those rolling their eyes or giving smirks at the notion of Noah being commanded to build a large barge. However, Noah knew of the upcoming cleansing and did not want these people to die. Many were his friends and relatives, and so he preached to them to repent. However, the people, even the seemingly "good" people, didn't hearken to his words. They weren't ready to leave the world behind and trust the Lord.

Noah continued to preach and said that those who would repent of their sins and believe in the warnings, were welcome to board the ark before the flood waters began to fall. After 120 years of preaching, the only people who stepped onto the ark were Noah and his family. Although there was room for many more people in the ark, only eight were saved. Redemption was offered to all who were willing to repent and believe. However, only few accepted the offer.

This story reminds me of when I felt my father's gentle hand on my back. After the plane had crashed, he could have been angry, but instead offered to build a new airplane. I could have continued my sobbing and yelling that hope was lost, but I trusted my father and knew he was a skilled craftsman. I knew he was capable of doing what he said he could do.

Do we trust that the Savior really is the path to redemption? Do we think He is capable of atoning for our sins? Do we trust that our Heavenly Father has provided a path to eternity for us? He provided a way for Noah to save himself, his family, his friends, and even his town.

Yes, only eight people were saved. I know a lot of good people in this world and to imagine only a portion of them making it in the end is heartbreaking. So, what happened? Why didn't Noah's friends and those in his own town believe him? The answer is that they were busy worshiping the world and not heeding the voice of a prophet. The great flood occurred before the internet, before video games, before cell phones, or before any other idols we now occupy our time with. We have allowed ourselves to become preoccupied with worldly distractions. Noah's people were also caught up in their own kind of distractions.

When I was running to save my father's glider, I was distracted by the wind and the bumpiness of the hard ground. However, I still did my best despite those distractions and my earthly father recognized that effort and showed me mercy.

When we are running this race of life, it is easy to get distracted by worldly things such as social media, work, politics, and even the time it takes deciding where to go out for dinner. However, the Lord will know of our intentions if we are doing the best we can. If we are seeking to uplift and guide others toward Christ instead of away from Him, God will also show mercy and offer us an ark. We too can build and then rebuild that which was broken. We can seek to create our own ark of safety.

Building Your Ark

As I was teaching a song to the primary children called, "Build an Ark,"[2] my testimony was strengthened that we have the power to access God's protection. It talks about how Noah was a prophet and he did not fear the teasing and looks of shame from the people. However, when he taught repentance, the people would not hear. So the Lord told him to build a boat. So he did. However, the magic of the song happens in the second verse. Instead of talking about Noah's ark, the verse is all about how we can build our own ark. I had to explain to the primary kids that the verse isn't about us actually building a boat, but more about what the ark represents. One little boy raised his hand and said, "Is it like when my mommy holds my hand when we go for a walk across the street?" I said, "Yes, it is much like that. When your mommy is holding your hand, it is to offer you protection. The ark in verse two is about building your own protection." "Ohhhhh, I get it now!" was his amazing response, smiling from ear to ear.

Then another child blurted out, "I still don't get it. How can we build that without having wood?" We all chuckled at their innocence and were also humbled by their meekness. "The ark of protection is not something you can see or touch like wood. You can build protection

---

2. Marianne P. Wilcock, "Build an Ark," *Friend*, Sept. 2010, 23.

against sin and temptation by doing things to build your courage in Christ and testimony of the gospel." I thought I had explained it clearly by now, but could see the looks of confusion on their faces.

Another teacher volunteered some more insight by sharing, "When we read the scriptures we gain a knowledge of Christ, God, and the Atonement. This offers protection to us. Instead of being scared when we make a wrong choice, we know we can repent." Brilliant! I then added, "We know Heavenly Father loves us and wants us to succeed. So, what are some other ways we can build an 'ark of protection'?" Many hands shot up and typical answers were given:

Read the scriptures
Say your prayers
Obey your parents
Go to church

We then discussed how each of those activities offers protection. Then we discussed what happens if we make a mistake? "We repent!" shouted one of the youngest children. Then I told them the story of me not catching my dad's plane and it ended up breaking. Some of them were sad. We discussed how he wouldn't be able to repair the plane, but could start over with a new one. This is similar to when we repent. Christ gives us a brand-new slate to work with, meaning a brand-new start and outlook on living the gospel.

Other arks of protection can come from seeking a personal relationship with Christ, serving others, and finding our own testimonies. The list goes on and on. You can create your own possibilities.

For me, one ark I have worked on building for nearly thirty years is having a traditional family dinner on Sundays. As my children have grown older, it can be harder to get all of us together. So we have a goal of at least two Sundays a month we are together breaking bread, discussing our goals and how to support one another. We aren't perfect, and Dean and I have had to step in to dissolve hurt feeling or disagreements. We have, however, decided we are family no matter what our political or other beliefs are. This dinner has provided us with belonging and support when many of my college students are needing it most. Just knowing you have a family—no matter how imperfect they are—that supports you, creates a safety net throughout life. We

CHAPTER THREE: HE OFFERS REDEMPTION

have also invited their roommates and friends over at times as well. The term "family" can mean many different things to different people and does not always have to mean related by blood. Although we are crazy loud, it has been worth the effort, including all the cleanup, to see my children bonding and growing closer at a time when we need it the most.

Our ark of redemption won't come without physical, emotional, and spiritual effort. But, if we are willing to weather the storm, our ark of redemption will guide us to safe waters. God does hear you and has not forgotten you. Once we turn off the voices of the world and tune into the powers of heaven, we will not fear man's judgment because we will know that the Savior of the World has created a path to redeem our souls.

Chapter Four

He Gives Us Spiritual Gifts

....

The Thing about Abish

"Oooooo, gross! You aren't really bleeding, are you?" shrieked Johnny Baker as we all sat astonished in our primary classroom. Roscoe was at it again. The teacher had left for a brief moment, likely to get help from the primary president as we were now completely out of control. We had just heard the story about Ammon cutting arms off his attackers all because he was defending King Lamoni's sheep. "Take that you sheep stealer!" Roscoe was engaged in a theatrical war pretending to be Ammon and grabbing everyone's arms, yanking them down towards the ground. "Ouch, you bully!" cried Amy as she slugged Roscoe in the offending arm.

I wish I could say I was the peacekeeper like Abish this day, but I joined in with Roscoe. Sorry to disappoint you. "You are wicked and now we take your arms!" I teasingly shouted as I jumped onto a chair, even amazing Roscoe who then jumped up to join me in our quest of ambushing the class. Johnny approached us pretending to hold a weapon in his hands and we then battled with our air swords, "Swish, clank, swish, Ug! You got me!" bellowed Roscoe as he grabbed his arm pretending to be wounded. With that, he closed his eyes and slowly fell forward, landing on top of Johnny as they both thudded onto the ground.

The entire class, seeing they weren't really hurt, burst into laughter as we all now fell to the ground pretending to have arms cut off from our bodies. Even Amy realized it was just a game and joined in the fun. Roscoe then pretended to squirt blood from his shoulder onto me. I freaked out just a little bit, you could say. I then jumped on top of him, tackling him as we rolled toward the door, all while shouting, "You are the grossest boy I know!" Roscoe threw me off of him and then jumped up from the ground, put his hands on his hips Peter Pan style, and said, "Why, thank you."

"Class! What in the heavens are you doing? Get into your seats this minute," commanded the primary president, Sister Fulmer, who had now entered the room. Sister Mitchell, our teacher, followed behind her, entering the room with aghast. Sister Mitchell was one of the kindest people I ever knew, but on this day Roscoe and I had pushed her over the edge. As we all calmed down and took our seats, I could see the primary president trying not to laugh as she composed herself in a seat up front, Sister Mitchell sat next to her. Sister Fulmer then told us we had to sit still for five minutes. We also couldn't talk as this was called the silent and reverent game. Once the five minutes was over, she had a calm discussion with us.

"So, what have we learned today?" she asked us CTR-B attendees, nine of us in total. We were silent. No one dared say the coolest thing we learned was that bad men had their arms cut off and that was likely all we would remember about the story. However, Sister Mitchell who was wise, collected herself and stated, "You didn't give me a chance to get to the good parts." We were wondering what could be better than bleeding appendages and looked at each other with curiosity. We gave various shoulder shrugs, with our hands facing upward in response, to show we were willing to listen. She then proceeded with

CHAPTER FOUR: HE GIVES US SPIRITUAL GIFTS

the remainder of the story of Ammon and how his preaching led to the conversion of King Lamoni and his people.

There was a part of the story that was only a few verses but caught my attention in an unusual way. Maybe it was because I had never heard the name before, or the fact it was the first time I had heard about a young, faithful girl saving Lamoni's servants. This girl's name is Abish. When Sister Mitchell read Alma 19:29, sharing how Abish wakened the Queen by touching her hand, I knew Abish was a prepared, valiant, and a faithful lady of God. I wanted to be faithful too, and decided to behave better in primary, at least for the rest of the class time that day.

Alma 19:29
And it came to pass that she went and took the queen by the hand, that perhaps she might raise her from the ground; and as soon as she touched her hand she arose and stood upon her feet, and cried with a loud voice, saying: O blessed Jesus, who has saved me from an awful hell! O blessed God, have mercy on this people!

The In-Between— We Are Modern-Day Abish

IT WASN'T UNTIL I BEGAN WORKING IN THE SCHOOLS THAT I UNDERstood the value of the shepherd. The shepherd protects the sheep and guides them to safety. This is a big job! I feel like a shepherd for my students and feel very protective of them as well. When students don't get along, it can be difficult discerning truth and how to best serve both sides of an issue. Abish's story follows two tribes and how they had to put God above stereotypes of each other and learn to find unity in the gospel.

The story begins when Ammon, a Nephite and one of the repented Sons of Mosiah, went on a mission to the Lamanites. The two groups weren't on great terms so bringing the gospel to the Lamanites would be very dangerous for Ammon. To his surprise, King Lamoni was very impressed with Ammon and asked him to be his son-in-law.

However, Ammon instead offered to be his servant. Huge points for Ammon. While Ammon was protecting King Lamoni's flocks, a group came to steal the sheep, but Ammon defeated them by cutting off the arms of their leaders. This is the part everyone remembers, but it gets even better!

As King Lamoni began to learn about Ammon's belief in the gospel, he fell to the ground and was thought to be dead. However, the queen knew he wasn't dead because he didn't stink, and she also trusted Ammon when he told her Lamoni would survive. Later, the king, queen, and servants all collapsed under the influence of the Spirit . . . that is, all except for Abish. Abish had been converted as a child when her father had a vision, and now was her chance to come out of silence and testify of the future Christ child and of God.

Abish touched the queen's hand and she was awakened. Then the queen touched Lamoni's hand and he was awakened. Why is this relevant? Abish used her spiritual gifts to bless the queen and then the queen blessed Lamoni. This is the only occurrence in the scriptures where two women were able to spiritually and physically heal their people. Abish had to put trust in a Nephite and show that God is bigger than tribal conflicts. The Lamanite queen is never personally named, but Abish is. Abish was a servant but never able to bare testimony of what she knew, until now. Now was the time all of her childhood training would matter, and she was able to share her spiritual gifts.

We are modern-day Abish and must be prepared to use our testimonies and gifts when key moments arise. These moments could be quiet, like performing simple acts of service. Or, these moments could be planned like putting your beliefs on social media, sticking up for what is right, even when it is not popular to do so. To have courage like Abish means trusting in the Holy Ghost to guide our actions and words. We cannot hide our spiritual gifts any longer. The world needs you to use your testimony and abilities as a light to the darkened world.

CHAPTER FOUR: HE GIVES US SPIRITUAL GIFTS

Using Your Spiritual Gifts

Spiritual gifts are gifts of power. Abish and the queen demonstrated how spiritual gifts can bless ourselves and the lives of others.

Gift one: Recognizing and receiving truth.

Abish believed her father's vision and the queen believed Ammon's testimony. Abish was converted to the Lord after her father had a vision. The queen, a Lamanite, never hearing the gospel before, believed in Ammon, a Nephite. Ammon said she was blessed because of her faith.

Alma 19:16
And it came to pass that they did call on the name of the Lord, in their might, even until they had all fallen to the earth, save it were one of the Lamanitish women, whose name was Abish, she having been converted unto the Lord for many years, on account of a remarkable vision of her father—

Alma 19:10
And Ammon said unto her: Blessed art thou because of thy exceeding faith; I say unto thee, woman, there has not been such great faith among all the people of the Nephites.

Acting on Faith

Ammon had told the queen her husband would eventually awaken, and he did. When King Lamoni shared his story with the household, he collapsed again. This time, the queen and servants collapsed too. Abish recognized this as an opportunity to help her people witness the power of God, so she acted in faith and "ran forth from house to house" (Alma 19:17), inviting her people to come and see.

Gift two: Showing courage in the face of danger.

Abish took a risk when she gathered the servants together, inviting them to see the power of God. After the servants argued saying it was a trick, they were overcome by the Spirit and collapsed. Likewise, the queen took a risk believing Ammon and also trusting in Abish.

We can follow Abish's example by inviting others to come unto Christ. This may be scary in a world that mocks faith and virtue. But I believe the time will come when hearts will be open to the truth whether it is because they are prepared or because an experience has humbled them. We can prepare ourselves as Abish did. Although she was silent for years, she was ready when the time was right. She still got pushback from her own people, but the queen knew of Abish's spirit and trusted her. I believe Abish prepared the queen to be open to the Spirit and she recognized the truth when Ammon spoke it.

Gift three: Having faith that God is a God of miracles.

Abish demonstrated a principle Elder Dieter F. Uchtdorf of the Quorum of the Twelve Apostles taught: "The difference between casual social contacts and compassionate, courageous discipleship is—invitation!"[1] Abish used her gift of faith inviting her friends to witness a miracle. The queen demonstrated her gift of faith not once, but twice. First when she knew Lamoni was not dead, only asleep, and secondly when she stretched forth her hand and woke her husband. She immediately began to testify of Jesus Christ and hers was the first testimony of the gospel many of those people had ever heard. King Lamoni also testified to the people and many of them were converted (Alma 19:30–33).

Acting on faith can take different forms. This could mean listening to a random prompting to turn down a different road. It could mean following a certain path of study at college or other form of higher education. It could mean testifying of the gospel to those who may reject you. The influence of righteous people is powerful. You are powerful. The people who heard Abish testify became converted to the Lord and never fell away, and it was their sons who became stripling warriors![2] The ripple effect was tremendous! Let's recap the impact one shared testimony can have. Although the ripple began even before Alma, we will start there:

---

1. Dieter F. Uchtdorf, "Your Great Adventure," *Ensign*, Nov. 2019, 88).
2. Elaine Dalton, "Love Her Mother," *Ensign*, Nov. 2011, 78.

CHAPTER FOUR: HE GIVES US SPIRITUAL GIFTS

- Alma to Alma the Younger
- Alma the Younger to/with the Sons of Mosiah
- Sons of Mosiah (Ammon) to King Lamoni (and Abish/queen)
- King Lamoni to his people
- His people to their sons, who became the stripling warriors

The ripple effect of goodness is all around us if we have ears to hear, hearts to feel, eyes to see, and bravery to act.

Don't Knock Me Over

There are many not of our faith who have also been given spiritual gifts. This concept of gifts is not just reserved for members, but gifts were given in the premortal existence, and it is up to us to uncover and share these gifts. One experience that comes to mind is about a student who shared his gifts abundantly. I will call him Carlos.

I was already tired and running late for work. I pulled into the parking lot and my favorite spot was already taken so I searched for the second-best parking spot, again it was taken. And so went the morning. I found a spot further from the front door than I had hoped as it began to rain. We needed moisture but I wondered why it couldn't have waited two more minutes for me to enter the building. I put my laptop bag over my head in hopes of avoiding damaging my newly straightened hair, but that only worked for the crown of my head and the rest my hair began to frizz up. I was still determined to have a good attitude.

I entered through the double doors with my purse in my right hand, laptop bag hung over my right shoulder. In my left hand I balanced a bucket of stress balls, and, hanging from my ring and pinky fingers, a plastic grocery bag holding my lunch. I walked carefully, hoping I didn't drop it nor the bucket. As I turned the corner to enter my classroom, I could see Carlos down at the other end of the long hallway.

He wasn't supposed to be out of class, but maybe he was just getting back from a bathroom break, so I didn't say anything. He was tall for his grade and often mistaken for an older student. He always had a friendly smile but was often bullied because he outweighed even the biggest kid by 50 pounds. Then, I heard him call, "Mrs. Porcelli!

Mrs. Porcelli," although, I pretended not to hear him. Then I see him coming toward me. At first, he walked and then he began to run full speed ahead.

He was now full-out charging towards me while calling my name. I froze in my tracks and tried to firmly square my feet so that he couldn't knock me over so easily. I dropped my purse and laptop bag to the ground and put my right hand out, trying to slow him down. And then it happened. As he barreled toward me, he skidded to a full stop, hitting my hand. He looked me in the eyes, oblivious to my panic, and exclaimed, "Oh Mrs. Porcelli! Where have you been? I have missed you!" My heart melted and he grabbed my arm and hugged it with all his might. While I was losing a bit of feeling in that arm from it being tugged on, I was overcome with joy that this young student who was so innocent shared his gift of optimism with me.

He could have been a bitter student, hating everyone for being so mean to him. But instead, he chose to share his light. In this way, he was like Abish. He chose to be like a warrior of goodness regardless of how others treated him. He was like Ammon. He chose to be open to the Spirit to know how to soften hearts. He was like the queen. He chose to continue being a leader, sharing goodness and later ending up on the student council. He was like King Lamoni.

I told the student, "Thank you. I missed you too!" with that he smiled and skipped back to class. The rest of the day seemed to go by smoothly until I had my hardest class come in for the counselor lesson. There was a certain 6th grade class whose teacher seemed to always be distracted with other things and would often leave me to handle their class's behaviors all by myself. I had to be sharp and organized.

Being prepared was my best tactic and I was hoping it worked. I wanted to continue sharing my spiritual gifts just as Carlos had earlier shared his gifts with me. Today, we were talking about growth mindset and being resilient. I shared a short video clip from the movie *Akeelah and the Bee*[3] when she is at the national spelling bee. I asked students to watch and see how Akeelah used a growth mindset to learn how to spell hard words. She learned in a unique way. After viewing the short clip, some students were impressed that she jumps rope and uses

---

3. *Akeelah and the Bee*, directed by Doug Atchison (Lionsgate, 2006).

CHAPTER FOUR: HE GIVES US SPIRITUAL GIFTS

rhythm to spell even the hardest of words. Then, I clicked the next slide displaying the adjective "argillaceous." That was the only word or picture on the slide. "Guess what we are going to do now?" Students looked curious as they knew I always had something fun but challenging up my sleeve. "We are going to have our own spelling bee and I am going to give you two minutes to practice this word before I call you up front." Oh boy, the kids sat up in their chairs, some groaned in complaint, and I played along saying, "Don't waste any time. Figure it out. Ready, Go!"

With that direction given, I discovered some kids using white boards to practice writing the word, some were just spelling it out loud with their eyes closed, and others were tapping or even jumping in rhythm. It is fun to help them use their anxious energy in a good way. Sometimes we fear feeling uncomfortable, but my goal is to teach students to channel this energy to help them rise to the occasion or challenge. Sometimes I am a stinker and I'll say things just to get the "eye rollers" to hop into action: "No pressure, but all of the first grade has already done this and many spelled the word correctly." One student heard this and said, "Is that why my little brother keeps challenging me to spell this word? This is where it came from?" I laughed and said, "I am happy to hear it meant so much to him. It is meant to be a fun experience. So, who is now ready to have some fun?" With that request called out, the students were cheering and begging for me to choose them first to come up front.

I thought I would relieve many students when I shared that it would be completely voluntary and no one "has to" come up front. However, not a single hand was lowered. Then they took turns coming up and standing in front of the class and spelling A-R-G-I-L-L-A-C-E-O-U-S. The rule was we were to clap even if they didn't spell it correctly, because we were applauding the "courageous courage" it took to do this. The teacher seemed dumbfounded how every student was able to spell this difficult word correctly, especially after only two minutes of practice, and asked me to share my secret with them. Realizing this teacher was a good human and likely just burned out, I shared, "Keep it fun for yourself. The students will feel that passion and be inspired to learn. You're doing great. You have an amazing class. Hang in there."

Over the years this teacher became one of my biggest advocates and told me their students looked forward to the lesson every month. I often hear students chant my name as I walk down the school hallway. I pretend it is because I am so cool, but realistically it is often because they know when I teach a lesson, they get a 30-minute break from math.

It took me so long to figure out how to share my spiritual gifts of light and love of learning. And some days I am so tired I forget the impact my attitude can have on these young learners. However, some days I bring it on and am on point! I hope these kids know their counselor loves them with all her heart.

We Can Make a Difference

No matter who you are or your circumstances, you can influence others for good through sharing your gifts and being willing to share your testimony of the gospel. Don't forget to invite others to partake as well. Even when the world may mock you for your beliefs, don't fear. You don't need to hide your belief, who you are, or wait for the best time to share your testimony with others. The time is now. The world hears so many negative voices on TV, social media, school hallways, and even through apps on their phone. I believe it is time we drown out the negative, replacing them with the positive messages of Christ as the Savior of the World. Not everyone will listen. Not everyone will accept. Not everyone will agree. However, those who are meant to hear will hear. You never know which stripling warrior is waiting for someone to share God's truth with them.

So, act in faith, invite others to come unto Christ and feel His love. Share stories and testimonies of the gospel. Be sensitive to the Spirit to know when it is time for you to listen—as Abish did for years—and when it is time for you to be brave—like Ammon after repenting to the Lord. Or, you can be like my student Carlos and spread light anywhere and everywhere you can. Pray for inspiration on how to share your gifts and testify of what is in your heart. With Heavenly Father and Jesus Christ at your side, you all make quite a tribe, and you can make a difference more than you realize.

Chapter Five
He Is the Good News

....

The Good News

"How come I'm the only one who ever gets in trouble?" Colton tearfully asked as he walked into our school Zen Den. He had been sent down by his teacher every day for the last four days. The Zen Den is a place our elementary students are allowed to come, for a short period of time, to calm down their brains and bodies and then be ready to focus back in the classroom. We set a sand timer for about 10 minutes and let them practice calming techniques. Sometimes students use our tools like coloring books, reading, or using sand, while other students just need someone to listen, so we do. It is their choice which tool to use to help manage their emotions. The counselor's job is to teach them capability and advise how to use their energy in the right direction.

"What happened?" I asked Colton who had pursed lips, tight fists, and looked like a raging bull ready for the attack. He then proceeded to tell me his side of the story and that he feels like no one ever likes him. He said he never gets picked at recess and he's always getting in trouble at home, always in trouble at school, and no one ever understands him. You get the picture. I then asked, "So what's the good news?" He looked puzzled. "Good news? There is never any good news . . ." On and on he went, talking about how life was so unfair and only unfair for him.

We all have had those days where nothing seems to go right. Maybe we compare ourselves to others who appear to have life put together neatly and seem to handle problems with ease. I have felt that way before and related to Colton on some level. However, I want to teach children to not focus or wallow on the negative. There is a time and place for that, but to also make room and make time for the good news. We need to celebrate the happy moments that often don't ever get recognized.

"Colton, I really like how your shirt matches your pants today," I complimented him, awaiting his surprised response. "Um, oh, thanks," he looked at me with his side-eye glare I often expect from him. "Colton, I have an idea. Let's talk about how awesome you are." This really got him going. He had wanted to complain about himself but knew I wasn't going to allow him to avoid math again just to come to the Zen Den and complain. "How awesome am I? There is nothing awesome about me." He pursed his lips and wouldn't look me in the eye. "Colton, I heard you opened the door for Mrs. Engel today. Is that true?" "Yah." "That is so awesome. You are a kind person. Thanks for doing that. Colton, thank you for talking with me in a calm manner. That takes true talent to be able to calm down so quickly. I can tell you have been practicing."

I don't know which big or little word was so magical, but with this he began to get alligator tears swelling up in his eyes as he leaned into me and gave me a big ol' side hug. I complimented him, "Thanks for being willing to trust me and talk with me. That means a lot." Then we walked over to the two student-sized massage chairs. We each sat down, individually reclined, and pressed the number seven (the best and smoothest mode of gentle lower back massage) and closed our eyes for a few minutes. After the sand timer ran out, he got up and said, "Thanks Mrs. Porcelli. See you around," and he jumped up, ran out the door, and skipped back to class.

I think sometimes we get so caught up in the negative, we forget how to be positive. It is easy to do when we have a hardship or heavy load. Some people can feel like they obtain energy by being negative, so they continue to do it. It hypes them up; they feel powerful and then recruit others, almost as if building unity by creating an army of negativity. We see negativity on the news, in social media, and if you ever deal with hormonal humans, you may be surrounded by skepticism (ha ha).

Unfortunately, we have become a world of naysayers posting about all the bad things including discouragement from having children, getting married, working hard in school, following Christ, being humble, seeking eternity, and the list goes on and on. The reality is, there are hard things that happen in life. There are things worthy of complaint. However, you were born a warrior. You were born as a child of God. You knew you would experience pain and sorrow, but yet you still shouted, "Hallelujah" in the premortal existence. We fought in the war in heaven so we could come to earth and experience sadness and learn from hardship. But, we also fought in the War in Heaven so we could experience joy, happiness, peace, and success! This peace is found in following Christ.

The In-Between— You Can Control the Narrative

YOU WILL KNOW MANY WHO APPEAR HAPPY AS THEY LEAVE THE gospel or follow a path contrary to the iron rod (1 Nephi 8). I view this growing multitude as the people in the large and spacious building, laughing and pointing fingers at the followers of Christ. However, in my experience, their "happiness" is often short term and often fake. They are stubborn and want you to join them by leaving the straight and narrow path. Misery loves company so they will say and do anything to convince you it is better in the large building. They are suppressing their conscience in a false sense of, "I have found a new or enlightened righteousness." They follow man's pleasures and walk on an easy, loud, gold-laden path. These same people who mock the righteous are afraid of doing the hard stuff. They are afraid to become humble and admit deep down they know their happiness is temporary and brings a false sense of security. Don't join the inevitable misery in the large and spacious building. Don't let them fool you into thinking a life of righteousness is hopeless. They are wrong.

It is time to spread the good news of the gospel. It is time to step up to the call of goodness, peace, happiness, and joy. It is time to shout, "Hallelujah, I follow Christ." As we become beacons of light, we must maintain humility and not appear self-righteous. It can be a difficult balance when you are full of so much joy. While I was chatting with Colton, I first needed to listen. Then, I could seek to understand. After this I could explore the good news with him. Once I could calm down his brain and get him out of his negative mindset, we could discuss the goodness of life. I could celebrate with him. We too can listen to those who complain and hear them out, but do not get caught up in their journey of bringing you into their personal misery. We can strive to help them out of their negative mindset, and finally explore the goodness of life and the goodness of the gospel.

Enter Sariah

I have often thought of Sariah, the wife to Lehi and mother to Nephi, Laman, and Lemuel. It must have been so hard when Lehi had his vision to leave all their worldly possessions behind and venture into the wilderness. Her life seems surrounded with good news, then bad news, then in-between news, then the cycle begins again. She was likely surrounded by doubt, fear, anger, and embarrassment. I can picture her self-righteousness former "friends" mocking her and making fun of her new lifestyle of simplicity and being poor, according to worldly terms.

Sariah's perseverance through incredible hardship is a testament to her faith in the Lord and Savior, Jesus Christ. She underwent a particularly challenging trial of faith when they had already left into the wilderness, and Lehi receives a new revelation that her sons have to return to Jerusalem to retrieve the brass plates (1 Nephi 3:4)

She knows her sons will face Laban, a wicked king, and their own lives will be in great danger. After much time had passed, Sariah was very distressed, fearing her sons had died, and she complained again about Lehi, that he had led them away from their comfortable lives and now her sons were dead; "Behold thou hast led us forth from the land of our inheritance, and my sons are no more, and we perish in the wilderness" (1 Nephi 5:2).

But, by the power of God, Laban fell down drunk and Nephi was able to imitate him, tricking the guards, and then obtain the plates from him. When Sariah's sons returned, safe and alive, it's no wonder that Sariah's "joy was full" and that she "was comforted" (1 Nephi 5:7).

Humbled by her momentary doubts, Sariah shared her newly strengthened testimony that the Lord had commanded Lehi to take his family and flee into the wilderness. She knew God had delivered her sons from the hands of Laban. But, hardships continued. They battled starvation and had to rely on the Liahona to guide them to "the more fertile parts of the wilderness" (1 Nephi 16:16). Sariah gave birth to more children along the journey and also received grandchildren.

Sariah endured what many mothers fear when rearing a large family: deep conflict among siblings. Laman and Lemuel continued to abuse Nephi and even attempted to kill him more than once. She witnessed her sons' hearts turn from the light and ultimately surrender to darkness. Yet, Sariah appears to have persevered, relying on faith to sustain her during many days of hardship.

Sariah's Good News

So, what's the good news? The good news is that she also witnessed the hand of God in their lives. Although she had her own story of doubt, she also has a story of triumph. She followed Christ no matter the physical or emotional cost. She witnessed her husband, Lehi, giving up all worldly goods to lead his family to God. She witnessed her children given an opportunity to hear from an angel. She witnessed the Liahona and how inspiration works among the righteous. She witnessed Nephi build a magnificent boat guiding them to the promised land.

Although Sariah's challenges were devastating, through her diligence and humility she witnessed the Lord's eternal love and compassion. Her family was fed when they were hungry. The Liahona worked when they were righteous. Her family's lives were spared multiple times. The family was eventually guided to a safe land prepared by God. Her testimony blesses the countless lives of those who read the Book of Mormon and relate to her as a mother, wife, or woman in the gospel.

I am sure there are many times she felt God did not hear her prayers. She was human and complained to her husband Lehi. However, her prayers to the Lord were answered, in His own timing. It was difficult for Sariah to see immediate blessings, but later she looked back on experiences with humbleness and a strengthened testimony. This is how God answers each of our prayers individually. Sometimes we get so caught up in the current situation we think all hope is lost. When we step back and view the experience from a different perspective, we can see God's hand in our lives at all times, and that our prayers were answered in unique ways.

We can look to the Lord as Sariah did and take upon us Christ's yoke. We can persevere and trust in God's plan as Nephi and Lehi did. We can be like Colton and appropriately calm our minds and learn from our behavior. We can focus on the good news and the opportunities we have to do better and be better. If we choose to learn and become humble, we have been promised that our burdens will be light and that we'll likewise "find rest unto [our] souls."

Matthew 11:29

Take my yoke upon you, and learn of me; for I am meek [gentle] and lowly [humble] in heart: and ye shall find rest unto your souls.

Celebrating the Gospel

I love celebrating the gospel of Jesus Christ. I don't think we can ever do enough when it comes to celebrating the life of our Savior. People are awesome. Sometimes we forget the amazing things people have experienced, done, or sacrificed. Sometimes we forget the amazing things Christ has done, experienced, and sacrificed. Let's join in celebrating the good news of the gospel.

CHAPTER FIVE: HE IS THE GOOD NEWS

For every sadness, there is always a turning point where light takes over the darkness. When Christ was on the cross and eventually died physically, the earth experienced darkness for three days. However, after the three days there was glorious light. Christ had been resurrected. It was time to celebrate. When angels saw Mary Magdalene at His sepulcher, they told her, "Go quickly, and tell his disciples that he is risen from the dead" (Matthew 28:7). Can you imagine how her heart must have felt to know that He lived? Then, Jesus appeared to her and said, "Go to my brethren, and say unto them, I ascend unto my Father, and your Father; and to my God, and your God" (John 20:17).

Mary experienced great sorrow when Jesus died, but that sorrow was lifted. She was rewarded for her devotion to Christ with His presence. She did go forth and share the good news that Christ lives.

When Christ appeared to the eleven apostles, He said, "Go ye into all the world, and preach the gospel to every creature" (Mark 16:15). Jesus was inviting them to share the good news. The Savior represents hope, redemption, and life. He wanted the apostles to share His word and to let others know that there is light in the world. That light is not just the gospel of Jesus Christ, rather the light is Jesus Christ Himself. He wants us to "have a desire to run and share the good news of His Resurrection with our friends and family. For 'he is not here; . . . he is risen!' (Matthew 28:6)."[1]

President Russell M. Nelson told patrons at the Rome Italy Temple dedication, "Things are going to move forward at an accelerated pace. . . . The Church is going to have an unprecedented future, unparalleled. We're just building up to what's ahead now."[2]

The "church" is you and me. It is the members. We are expected to celebrate the good news, meaning that soon all our labors will bear fruit. The hard work we have put into being worthy, being diligent, having faith, and following the prophet will bring forth the truth to those who are waiting for the opportunity to worship God without

---

1. "Mary Shares the Good News," *Easter Study Plan: Mary Magdalene—A Chosen Witness*, Sunday Apr. 17, 2022, www.churchofjesuschrist.org/study/manual/easter-plan-mary-magdalene-2022.
2. Irinna Danielson, "The most important change that has to happen for the Church's 'unprecedented future,' *Church News*, 29 Mar. 2019, www.thechurchnews.com.

fear or repression. So many around the world need our light. They need the light of Christ. The good news is that the Holy Ghost has been preparing their hearts for a time such as this. It is now. Although we have experienced recessions, pandemics, social conflicts, and political unrest, we are survivors. We can learn from the past to create a bright and hopeful future.

Our main job is to turn our lives over to the work. President Ezra Taft Benson said, "Men and women who turn their lives over to God will find out that He can make a lot more out of their lives than they can. He will deepen their joys, expand their vision, quicken their minds, strengthen their muscles, lift their spirits, multiply their blessings, increase their opportunities, comfort their souls, raise up friends, and pour out peace."[3]

We have been offered so many blessings by doing so little. All we are asked to do is follow Christ's example and trust that God has laid out a plan for us. We are to follow the plan to the best of our abilities. Don't get upset if you fall off the path along the journey. The path will always be there. You know where it is. Put all your efforts to getting back onto that path. Once on that path, hold to the rod with all your might. Don't worry about the people in the great and spacious building, they aren't holding onto the rod. You are.

In Lehi's vision of the Tree of Life he saw people fall away from the rod because they lost focus. They got distracted by those off the path calling to them (1 Nephi 8:21–28). You have everything you need to keep your focus and hold onto that rod with all your might. Look to the tree and press on.

What's in It for You?

By holding to the rod, we create even more good news. The teachings of The Church of Jesus Christ of Latter-Day Saints carry with it many opportunities to experience joy, peace, and happiness. Membership has its cost (time, effort, sacrifice), but also offers a huge reward. A few

---

3. Ezra Taft Benson, "Jesus Christ—Gifts and Expectations," Brigham Young University devotional, 10 Dec. 1974, speeches.byu.edu.

CHAPTER FIVE: HE IS THE GOOD NEWS

of the rewards we can partake of by accepting the gospel include but are not limited to:

Gospel Principle	Blessing
The Resurrection	Knowledge that Christ lives and is watching over us.
Repentance	The opportunity to seek forgiveness.
Baptism by Emersion	Opportunity to repent and be baptized. We are given a clean slate by the power of the priesthood.
Families are of God	Opportunity to be sealed for eternity to your family. We are the only gospel with sealing powers to unite families after death.
Eternal Life	Knowing that death is not the end. We will be resurrected and so will our loved ones.
Temples	The opportunity to serve in the temples and to do ordinances for ourselves and our ancestors. The temples grant peace and tranquility away from the world.
Plan of Happiness	Knowing who we are, where we came from, why we are here and where we are going (or at least where we are striving to go!).
Holy Ghost	The opportunity to have the Holy Ghost as our constant companion and guide
Jesus Christ	Knowledge of who Jesus Christ actually is: He is the Savior, our mentor, our brother, and our friend.
The Spirit of God	Multiple opportunities to feel the Spirit and witness how the Spirit manifests, confirms, and influences our lives.
Book of Mormon	Another testimony of Jesus Christ. Guidebook to help us along this journey of life.

Primary	The awesome primary songs we get to sing and then choose to learn from and invite the Spirit into our lives.
	Primary teachers who give weekly gospel lessons and help us create relationships with trusted adults.
Youth Programs	We are given mentors and leaders to help us.
	Opportunities to give talks, serve, and have weekly activities.
	Fun, spiritual camps or conferences, like trek, girls camp, high adventure, etc. (I vote we need a camp for adults too, but no one seems to listen to me . . . ha ha!)
Modern Prophets	Leaders who focus on the Spirit and being inspired to share messages of hope and goodness with the world.
	Having a prophet on earth who is a witness of and speaks for God.

The list of blessings of the gospel could go on and on. What would you add? Why?

Let's celebrate our beliefs, our sacrifices, and the joy the gospel brings to our lives. President Gordon B. Hinckley advised, "Carry on. Things will work out. If you keep trying and praying and working, things will work out. They always do. If you want to die at an early age, dwell on the negative. Accentuate the positive, and you'll be around for a while."[4]

Just like Colton who had complained in the Zen Den before realizing his life wasn't so bad, or Sariah doubting and then gaining a testimony through so much sacrifice, Christ knows we each have our individual journeys. Those journeys can be difficult. Life was not meant to be easy. However, life was not meant to be torture either. He died on the cross so that we can have agency, make mistakes, repent, and then do better. He is the good news. He wants us to find joy in the journey, peace in Christ, and happiness throughout life.

---

4. Gordon B. Hinckley in Sheri Dew, *Go Forward with Faith* (Salt Lake City, UT: Deseret Book, 2001), 423.

Chapter Six

He Helps Us Become Self-Reliant

....

Pop Goes the Weasel

"Pop goes the weasel!" The sound grew louder and louder as my heart began to pump faster. I couldn't get the song out of my mind and I knew I had to try to find him. I grabbed the three shiny silver dimes off the top of my dresser, put them into my front pocket, ran out the door, and hopped onto "Old Bo," my trusty, rusty, green-colored bicycle. My bike pedals couldn't seem to go fast enough as my little legs were pushing round and round. The white van was pulling further away and my heart was sinking. "I must catch up," I kept telling myself as the wind blew against my efforts. I could hear the music beginning to fade. "Oh no! I can't make out the notes anymore," I cried to myself.

My "Old Bo" had an amazing, shiny green, banana-shaped seat on it. It even had a white stripe on the sides to match the handlebar covers. I was so proud I had learned to ride this bike and had now become an expert. At least I was an expert in my own mind. This bicycle had become my best friend and accompanied me on many journeys to and from friend's houses, late night neighborhood hide-and-seek gatherings, to now, chasing down the ice cream man who had often driven through our small east-side neighborhood.

All of my friends had bragged about how their parents had bought them the new flavor of ice cream: mint chocolate chip. I had to try it. The ice cream man didn't seem to really care about kids or making money because he put more effort into driving recklessly as he turned down another street. By this time, I had made it around the corner and could still see the brightly decorated truck just ahead. I was gaining on him. "Faster, must go faster," I kept thinking. I didn't give up and Old Bo was doing it! We were catching up and I was beginning to close the gap. The truck then slowed down as it rounded another corner and I knew I could make it to him in time. He just had to see me in the rear-view mirror. I was excellent at turning corners, or so I thought.

Then the devastation happened. *Crash!* I found myself in the gravel on the side of the road. I looked down to see my knee bleeding profusely. I wailed and wailed but no one came to rescue me. "What happened?" I thought. "I was so close." Once the tears cleared my eyes, I examined my surroundings and realized I had forgotten about the new speed bump they had just put into the neighborhood. How could they do that when they knew there is a possibility of the ice cream man going much too fast down the street? My childlike mind felt betrayed.

But now I needed help. Couldn't anyone hear my cries? I was bellowing out like a donkey, surely someone would hear me. My knee hurt profusely, and I carefully hopped back onto my bike. Old Bo was now scratched up and my banana seat was twisted. I tried to push it back into place the best I could and examined the frame. Everything else seemed intact. It hurt to pedal but I knew I had to do it. I could ride "Old Bo" all the way home or I could find help a bit closer. As a child I was always reactive and never a thinker. This time was no different, but I like to view it as being led by inspiration. I found my

CHAPTER SIX: HE HELPS US BECOME SELF-RELIANT

bike taking me down an odd street and didn't really know why I was going that direction until I saw a familiar home. The home belonged to Bishop Lybbert. We were taught in primary to seek out trusted adults and he was an adult that was gentle and kind. However, it was the middle of the day and I knew he wouldn't be home, but likely his wife would be home. She was just as nice as her husband and seemed so pleasant at church.

I dumped the bike on their lawn and shamefully climbed up the steps to their front door. I rang the doorbell and waited. Then, I saw Sister Lybbert enter the doorway. When she saw me she knew I needed help. "Don't you want to go to your own house for a band aid?" she asked, due to the fact I only lived a few streets away. "No, I want *you* to take care of me," I cried, wiping away a few tears, as she looked surprised. She was a little hesitant but eventually invited me in and cleaned up my wound then put on a fresh band aid. Although I felt better physically, I kept thinking of how I would never be able to taste mint chocolate ice cream. I was disheartened at the thought. Sister Lybbert then asked if she could give me a treat to help me calm down a bit. Well, well, well, things were definitely beginning to look up.

I sat down at her Formica table in her kitchen that was decorated with flowery wallpaper. Then she opened her freezer and pulled out some ice cream. I figured getting any kind of ice cream was a huge win at this point. Then she asked, "I have a new kind of ice cream I found at Reams grocery store. Do you want to try it?" Of course, I said, "Yes." Then she brought a small bowl with a child size spoon to the table and placed it in front of me. The ice cream was such an odd color of ice cream and it had black specs in it. It was light green in color and the smell was different than I was used to. Then, I realized that there in front of me was offered a free bowl of the new flavored mint chocolate chip ice cream! I dug into the ice cream like nobody's business.

With the first bite I wasn't quite sure if I liked it or not. It definitely was minty and that was new to me. But, once I realized the black specs were chopped up chocolate chip pieces, I ate every last bite and even licked the bowl. Sister Lybbert laughed and then sent me on my way.

As we get older, we can often forget childhood experiences, but I have always remembered this experience quite clearly. It meant so much to me to have someone, other than my parents, that I could trust to help me. While it is important to expand our circle of relationships and know who to go to in times of need, it can be difficult to ask for help sometimes. However, we must realize that some people don't know we need help and will never know until we tell them. This is why children are so great. They often have no problem asking or letting people help them. I think Heavenly Father wants us to have a childlike spirit for many reasons, including learning how to be humble, thankful, innocent, willing to take direction, being open to new ideas, and the ability to reach out for help when needed.

The Savior teaches in the gospel of Matthew, "Except ye be converted, and becomes as little children, ye shall not enter into the kingdom of heaven" (18:3) and "Suffer little children, and forbid them not, to come unto me: for of such is the kingdom of heaven" (19:14).

What does it mean to become as a little child? When I reflect upon my experience with Sister Lybbert, I am reminded that I sought her out. I didn't wait for someone else to save me. I had to make an effort, express my needs, and then trust she could help me. Our relationship with the Savior is like this. We make an effort to solve our problems, seek Him to assist us in those efforts, and then trust that He can and will help us.

Self-Reliance with a Little Bit of Help

A valuable lesson I have learned is that others often have no idea what you are going through unless we make them aware of our needs. It doesn't mean they don't care about you, but rather that they have a lot on their own plates to take care of as well. They likely are just swimming the best they can in their own sea of life. They cannot be expected to read our minds, so we need to let them know when we need assistance. This could look like you talking with a church leader or a neighbor, counselor, friend, etc. The point is, just reach out. If that person doesn't help you, then reach out to someone else. But don't give up on the gift the Lord has given you, meaning the opportunity of having loving and caring relationships with others who can assist us along the journey.

CHAPTER SIX: HE HELPS US BECOME SELF-RELIANT

When we experience stress, there is a hormone released in our brains called oxytocin. This is known as the hugging hormone because it instinctually makes us want to reach out for help from others, promoting trust, bonding, and attachment. To understand the significance of this God-given hormone, let's discuss a real-life situation. Do you remember what you felt like the last time you heard a baby cry? You were likely alerted, maybe uncomfortable, or even a little sad. Babies are born with a will to survive. Their cries help release endorphins to help calm their distress and also signals oxytocin in anyone who hears their plea for help. Upon hearing the sometimes-shrieking wail of a baby, we may have our heart skip a beat or we might look around to see who is going to attend to the infant. Our bodies want someone to respond to this call for help. We want the crying to stop and for the baby to be okay. Our body chemistry is made not only to send "help signals" but also made to receive help signals and then attend to these S.O.S. calls. We were meant to be on this journey together.[1]

When we decide to stop reaching out to others, that is a learned behavior, not instinctual behavior. Whether or not you decide to face challenges yourself, or decide to instead reach out for assistance, can often be related to our past experiences. Our personal views about trusting others to help us when we are in need highly depends on whether you have or have not been helped in the past. Children who do not have their emotional needs tended to, often learn to sooth themselves. This is good, and not so good at times. It is great to give parents a break when an infant can solve their own problems. However, if they never receive emotional support, they often grow up and learn to not trust others. It is a tricky balance for parents to know when to intervene and help and when to let kids solve their own dilemmas. On the other hand, when parents use discretion and know when to assist their children and when to let them solve their own problems, a child can learn to trust others and also learn to trust themselves.

This is how the Lord works. He wants us to turn to Him for His guidance, but we are to be self-reliant in solving problems. He lets

---

1. "What happens to a mother's brain when she hears her baby crying?" *Mas & Pas: The Parenting Network,* accessed Oct. 2022, https://masandpas.com/what-happens-to-a-mothers-brain-when-she-hears-her-baby-cry/.

us stumble and sometimes fall, but He will be there coaching us on how to pick ourselves back up and move forward. When we withdraw ourselves from the aid of the Lord, we create what is called spiritual distance. The more we feed into hurt feelings, anger, and disappointment, the greater the spiritual distance. This is how hearts become hardened. People build walls of protection so they cannot be hurt again. They lock up their hearts and stop listening to promptings, counsel from prophets, and stop talking with God.

I have seen many give up on the Lord, church, friendships, and other relationships because they feel like they have been forgotten. It can be difficult to remain faithful if you feel unnoticed, unwanted, unneeded, or unattended to and misinterpret those feelings as rejection from God. God does not reject you. He loves and needs you. We love and need you. You will never know who is waiting to get to know you and learn of your talents, thoughts, experiences, and testimony if you don't share them. The gospel is a gospel of love and unity. Please don't give up.

Forgiveness in All the Right Places

We all likely know someone who has allowed their hearts to harden over hurt feelings, feeling forgotten, being offended, the list goes on. I think Christ wants us to have a childlike heart as one who easily forgives and moves on. Forgiving others doesn't mean we think what someone did or didn't do is okay, but rather means we release the power that grudges can often hold over our hearts. I could have held a grudge over all the ice cream drivers in the world, but I chose to move on. I know that may be a trivial example and I am not trying to make light of what hardships we often experience in life. But rather it is an example of how easily grudges can turn our hearts away from other people and relationships. Unfortunately, holding onto grudges can also lead to turning our hearts away from our relationship with Jesus Christ.

People often harbor grudges when they have unmet expectations in their ward or in the gospel. This could range from not getting the calling you want in your ward, to not getting your prayers answered in the time or way you had hoped. Sometimes the grudge is slowly developed over time through a series of small events such as when other humans say or do hurtful things. You may have been offended by a neighbor or upset when your child has an argument with another child in the area. It is common to have hurt feelings when we don't get noticed or included and take it even more personally when our children don't get included or invited to activities or gatherings. We feel left out and like we don't fit in. We can easily translate not fitting in socially to also not fitting in with the gospel. We all have something we are disappointed in during our lifetime. If we let the disappointment continue to swell, the once seemingly small grudge seems to quickly grow bigger. Then it becomes easier to stay home from church, slightly back off on your calling, or even find fault with gospel leaders and teachings. You likely know someone this has happened to, maybe even to you.

Don't let someone else's actions (or inactions) dictate how you follow Christ. Your testimony is your testimony. When you face the Lord, He is not going to ask about your neighbor's sins or even their triumphs. You will be reporting on *your* life and how you chose to live it. Let go of grudges. Forgive others. Forgive yourself. Allow Christ to work on you as an individual. This will allow your mind to be open to new possibilities and a great love for not just yourself, but for others as well.

What Is Expected from You?

God has asked us to serve each other. The first and greatest commandment is to "Love the Lord thy God." The commandment "Love thy neighbor as thyself" is the second commandment and "like unto" the greatest commandment. This doesn't always mean your exact next-door neighbor, but rather those you associate with and maybe even those you have yet to associate with.

Matthew 22:37–40
Jesus said unto him, Thou shalt love the Lord thy God with all they heart, and with all thy soul, and with all thy mind.

This is the first and great commandment.

> *And the second is like unto it, Thou shalt love*
> *thy neighbor as thyself.*
>
> *On these two commandments hang all the law and the prophets.*

We are physically wired to serve others. Eva Ritvo, a doctor of psychiatry, says, "Neuroscience has demonstrated that giving is a powerful pathway for creating more personal joy and improving overall health. . . . Dopamine, serotonin, and oxytocin make up the *Happiness Trifecta*. Any activity that increases the production of these neurochemicals will cause a boost in mood."[2]

Bottom Line: When we help others, we physically feel better.

But What about Self-Reliance?

"Doesn't self-reliance mean we are to take care of ourselves?" I have often heard this question when discussing this topic. Self-reliance is about putting in your own good works and not leaving that work to others, but is also about being prepared to serve the Lord and to serve your neighbors. Once you take care of you and your own family's needs, the goal is to have enough "of you" left to feel you can also offer service to others. However, there is a difference between taking over versus teaching someone how to take care of themselves. We realistically teach children to tie their shoes, teens how to budget money, and adults how to be resourceful to meet their needs. "The saying goes that if you give a man a fish, you have fed him for a day, but if you teach him to fish, you have fed him for a lifetime."[3]

---

2. Eva Ritvo, "The Neuroscience of Giving: Proof that helping others helps you," *Psychology Today,* 24 Apr. 2014, www.psychologytoday.com.
3. Adam C. Olson, "Teach a Man to Fish," *New Era,* June 2011, 19.

CHAPTER SIX: HE HELPS US BECOME SELF-RELIANT

The In-Between— What Does This Mean to Me?

ONE OF THE GREATEST WAYS TO SERVE IS TO HELP OTHERS BECOME emotionally and spiritually self-reliant by trusting in the Lord.

Proverbs 3:5–6
Trust in the Lord with all thine heart; and lean not unto thine own understanding.

In all thy ways acknowledge him, and he shall direct thy paths.

I definitely pride myself in being self-reliant. I don't need a lot of hand holding when it comes to my daily work or tasks. However, I have learned that self-reliance doesn't actually mean doing everything "on my own." Spiritual self-reliance includes faith in and dependence on the Savior.

2 Nephi 4:34–35
O Lord, I have trusted in thee, and I will trust in thee forever....

Yea, I know that God will give liberally to him that asketh.

"God will give liberally to him that asketh!" What an amazing promise. However, we have to first trust in the Lord. That is the part where we reach out and ask Him for help. Elder M. Russell Ballard spoke during a fireside at Brigham Young University explaining that we need to ask and then be faithful, using our testimony as an anchor:

Ask your Heavenly Father to bless you with faith and courage, and He will help you endure any challenges you may face. He will help you overcome loneliness, feelings of desperation and hopelessness, setbacks of a personal, emotional, financial, and even spiritual nature. He will strengthen you when you are simply feeling overwhelmed by all of the demands for your time and attention. He will give you the ability to serve faithfully in every assignment you receive from your local Church leaders. Your faith and your knowledge of the restoration of the gospel will give you the strength to be faithful and true to the covenants you have made with the Lord and to share your strengths and talents gladly to build up the kingdom of God here on the earth.

Brothers and sisters, your testimony of Jesus Christ is the most important anchor that you can have to help hold you steadfast and immovable to principles of righteousness, regardless of the challenges and temptations that may come in the future.[4]

When I crashed on my bike, I'm sure that if enough time had passed, I would have likely pulled myself together, made it home, found my own band aid, and would have been very self-reliant taking care of my wounds. However, the self-reliance I learned was putting trust in following my heart, which led me to Sister Lybbert's home. I needed more than physical resilience but rather needed some emotional support in the form of a kind woman offering a band aid and bowl of chocolate mint ice cream.

We need to feel the Savior's love. We may even crave it. We need to put our trust in Him that once we have put forth all our efforts, He will make up for the rest. We need to ask in faith that He can help us bridge the gap between heaven and earth. That is the anchor to our soul I believe Elder Ballard was speaking of.

Enter Joseph

When I think of the phrase "self-reliance with a little bit of help," I think of the prophet Joseph Smith. This fourteen-year-old boy first had faith, then asked for help when seeking which church to join, and then trusted our Father in Heaven would answer his plea. I don't know many fourteen-year-olds that would be self-reliant enough to research multiple religions, journey to other church buildings to discuss religious topics with other priests to gather data, and then enter the woods all by themselves to ask God such a serious and meaningful question. He may not have known it then, but Joseph was practicing the Scientific Method, and blessedly found his theory to join none of those churches. The "little bit of help" really is "a lot of help" when we

---

4. M. Russell Ballard, "Anchor to the Soul," Brigham Young University fireside, 6 Sept. 1992, speeches.byu.edu.

CHAPTER SIX: HE HELPS US BECOME SELF-RELIANT

factor in the Lord. Joseph needed to be self-reliant, but also allow the Lord to help him along his journey of faith.

Joseph's family were sturdy pioneers and hard workers. The Smith family knew how to put forth physical effort to obtain a goal. In 1840, Joseph wrote, "Let the Saints remember that great things depend on their individual exertion."[5]

Joseph's younger brother William stated:

> *We cleared sixty acres of the heaviest timber I ever saw. We had a good place. We also had on it from twelve to fifteen hundred sugar trees, and to gather the sap and make sugar and molasses from that number of trees was no lazy job. We worked hard to clear our place . . . If you will figure up how much work it would take to clear sixty acres of heavy timber land, heavier than any here, trees you could not conveniently cut down, you can tell whether we were lazy or not, and Joseph did his share of the work with the rest of the boys.*[6]

Joseph was what I call a "mover and shaker," meaning he knew when it was time to get things done and when it was time to be calm and put trust in the Lord. He certainly was self-reliant "with a little bit of help" when translating the Book of Mormon. He used seer tools, including the Urim and Thummim, in translating the Book of Mormon and in obtaining other revelations.[7] He had to practice faithfulness for the Urim and Thummim to work. When he was not faithful, the instruments did not work (see D&C 17:1–2). This concept can relate to the modern day as we want blessings from the Lord, but understand that we need to hold up our end of the deal as well.

We likely know someone who likes to complain a lot when their needs are not being met. Yet, it often seems that these same people do none of the helping. I know I have been this person at times. I

---

5. "How Good and How Pleasant It Is . . . to Dwell Together in Unity," *Teachings of Presidents of the Church: Joseph Smith* (2007), 276.
6. J. W. Peterson, "Another Testimony: Statement of William Smith, Concerning Joseph, the Prophet," *Deseret Evening News*, Jan. 20, 1894, 11; https://newspapers.lib.utah.edu/ark:/87278/s60c5qx0/1626557.
7. "Urim and Thummim," Bible Dictionary, churchofjesuschrist.org; See also JS—H 1:35.

have caught myself being a main complainer. The reality is you will encounter many complainers in life. A big reason people complain is because they may feel stuck, helpless, or even scared; but they can feel a sense of unity or power when they complain. It gives us an excuse to do "nothing" instead of putting forth positive effort when dealing with a situation.

However, the gospel of Jesus Christ is a gospel of action. Joseph knew this and He took action. He made effort, worked through trials and took corrections from the Lord to translate the golden plates. Now, we have the Book of Mormon to lead and guide us back to our Father in Heaven. When we lessen the complaining and take that saved energy and put it towards good works, Heavenly Father will perform miracles in our lives.

Spiritual Self-Reliance

There is a time for physical effort and there is a time for emotional effort. When we combine our physical and emotional efforts, that is where spiritual self-reliance resides. When the body and mind unite, we are awakening our soul to listen for inspiration from the Lord.

One of my favorite places to practice prayer and meditation is in the woods. There is something freeing about listening to aspen trees when the wind catches their leaves just right and they sound like crackling popcorn. When I hear the birds chirping or a gentle creek gliding by, I feel all is well in the world. It is my escape. You likely have an escape too. This could be the beach, your room, a pool, the chapel, wherever you feel connected with the Spirit.

I like to focus on my physical body first so I can relax and not have my body's quirks later distract my mind. My meditation consists of deep breathing techniques along with physical techniques to calm my mind. Then, I can listen for the Spirit and listen to what my soul is saying to me. This may sound like a weird concept, but I have always known my soul and how to access this connection with God. It can take practice, but gets easier the more we pray, meditate, and listen to our bodies and minds.

Unfortunately, there have been times my physical body takes over and I don't feel physically nor mentally healthy. This is when I need to ask for help from the Lord. This could also mean reaching out for help from experts. This could mean paying closer attention to the Word of Wisdom and being careful what we allow to enter our bodies. This could mean paying closer attention to social media, apps, movies, etc. and what we allow to enter our minds. Once we take accountability for what we can control, the Lord will help us with what we cannot control.

The Prayer Factor

The Lord knows each of our individual needs. He hears our individual prayers. He knew Brother Joseph needed divine guidance, even seer tools, to help translate the Book of Mormon. He knows of your physical needs. He knows of your emotional needs. He knew I wanted mint chocolate chip ice cream that special day. However, he also expects us to make an effort and be self-reliant with the things we can handle. Don't hold yourself back. Joseph had to search, ponder, and pray. Why would any less be expected of us? When you have a difficult issue you are dealing with, you too can use the same method as Joseph, trusting that the Lord will make up for the difference.

Chapter Seven

He Is Merciful

....

Meet Popo

The sweltering sun cheered on the sweat dripping from their dirt-filled scalps, sliding down sunburned cheeks, and finally plopping onto the dirt below. The exhausting heat was unbearable, but they couldn't let it distract them from their mission to help these starving souls. Hopeful faces glared forward in line, some with bruises up and down their bodies, sullenly awaiting their turn. Their bellies had been hungry for many days and it was the mission of New Hope Ministry to help calm their aches, even a little, at least once a week. However, the only food they could offer that day was a scoop of white rice with one small slice of mango fruit. It wasn't nourishing, but it would have to do. Glen, the leader of the volunteers, knew they had to ration smaller portions than usual to have enough to feed all that made the journey that day. The silence from the adults in line was deadening as their eyes grew more sullen with each passing day.

However, today was different from the rest because some new kids showed up and anxiously entered the long line. This new group of orphans ran in a pack of seven ranging in age from four to fourteen along with one dog, named Butuk, whose ribs were protruding from his belly. The fourteen-year-old was the one responsible for keeping them safe and looking out for their needs. Unfortunately, there was never enough to meet anyone's needs.

The volunteers gathered the white foam food boxes to put the rice in each week. Luckily, today they had someone donate 20 mangos so that they could offer one slice to about 100 people. It would have to be enough. It was a sweet dessert for the humble group who had gathered in hopes of something other than just the weekly rice box.

One orphan in particular caught Glen's eye. He was only four years old but could speak quite well and had not lost his sparkle of hope yet. "I'm new," he exclaimed as he jumped in front of an older boy in line. "Hey, that's my spot. Go to the back where you belong," shouted an angry patron. The volunteers looked at each other with concern, knowing they had to keep things calm or they couldn't meet at this spot anymore. "Baashir, it's his first time. Maybe just this once?" Glen was hopeful but cautious. "Fine, but next time go to the back and wait your turn," Baashir responded, sounding half angry and half defeated. Baashir was older and also an orphan. He had been coming to this spot on a weekly basis for over a year. He was good at hiding when he needed protection, but Glen always knew where to find him if needed. New Hope Ministry depended on Baashir to be a leader and to guide others to their safe community.

The little boy was now gleaming with pride as he jumped forward to pick up his food box. "What's your name, little one?" a volunteer named Alice asked while she scooped rice into the tray. "Popo!" he shouted proudly while pointing to himself, grinning from ear to ear. "Popo is a very nice name," Glen told him. "Did your mommy name you that for a special reason?" Glen asked before catching himself. Glen looked down sorrowfully because he knew better than to ask any of the children that. What was he thinking?

CHAPTER SEVEN: HE IS MERCIFUL

Popo never knew his father and his mom was tortured and murdered during a terrorist attack two years prior. Popo had wandered the streets as a toddler for months before finding shelter a few hours away. When the shelter was destroyed by the Taliban, the survivors scattered. Popo was one of them. Luckily, this new group he was hanging out with had migrated over the years to the north, where New Hope Ministry was stationed.

Alice then surprised Popo by putting a piece of the fruit on top of his rice. "Oh boy!" he exclaimed and ran off. "Say thanks you little beast!" yelled Baashir. "It's okay," Alice said with a half grin on her face. "He will learn manners a little bit more each time he comes." The rest of the volunteers didn't think much of the incident and continued serving the food boxes. Then Glen looked down to the end of the line and noticed someone who was acting quite peculiar.

Popo had gone to the back of the line to get seconds, along with a few newcomers, sliding in quickly behind him. The problem? New Hope Ministry doesn't offer second helpings as they often ran out of food and had to turn people away. Pakistan is a hard place with so many in need. They had to run a tight program in order to stay afloat. Popo appeared to be patiently waiting his turn as the wind began to swirl with spatters of dust settling on top of some of the foam containers. However, the dirt didn't seem to bother anybody as they were now used to it, often finding it settled at the bottom of their boxes.

On this day, the wind also kicked up the smell from the garbage that had laid on the ground for months. It wreaked like molding cabbage, but there wasn't anything anyone did about it. Small groups of people began to form under sparse trees, which offered a tiny bit of shade, as they dined on their feast together. As energy began to lift, so did their spirits and their chatter grew louder. Excitement was in the air over the surprise mango fruit. You could see eyes widen as they perked up and smiled at each other discussing the sweetness, and of course conversing about the week's events.

New Hope Ministry still had about ten people to feed in line and only nine food boxes left. When Popo made his way up in the line it became his turn again, in front of four other patrons. "Popo!" Glen exclaimed. "What do you think you are doing back in line?" With this question Popo looked confused and gasped, "Huh? But how did you recognize me?" Glen glanced down to get a closer look. He then realized the trick Popo performed to acquire a second food box. Popo had found some red lipstick and smeared it all over his face in hopes of disguising himself. Glen chuckled, as he lifted his arm to wipe some sweat from his brow. The other volunteers giggled but knew they now had a somber decision to make. There were only four food boxes and five people left in line, including Popo.

"Popo," Glen questioned sternly, "where is your food box we already gave you?" Popo looked ashamed as he glanced at his dirty feet that had been shoeless for about a year. "Um," he hesitated slightly, pushing some more dirt around with his big toe. He made a full circle design in the ground and then hesitantly continued, "I gave it to my dog." Popo then shyly looked up at Glen awaiting his response. Then he looked to the other volunteers, this time making eye contact with Alice. Popo then shifted his gaze somewhere in the distance, as his bottom lip began to poke out. He tried hard to fight back his tears. Batuk waited proudly by his side, panting heavily.

"Popo! Why did you give the food box to your dog?" Alice gasped at the thought. After hearing this question, Popo took a deep breath and pursed his lips as he blurted out, "Because he is my family too!" With that response the volunteers' hearts expanded, growing a few sizes, making the one box rule a bit harder to follow. What would they do? They could teach Popo a lesson and let him go hungry, that would be fair. Or, they could give him another food box, showing mercy, but another person in line wouldn't be fed that day.

Just then an older woman at the very back of the line spoke up, "Give him my food box." "But, Atafa you also deserve to eat today!" Glen reminded the elderly woman. "I had food yesterday," Atafa announced confidently and continued, "I would be honored to let him have my rice and mango today." With that, Popo smiled, accepted the food box, and ran off to show the others in his group. Batuk barked, wagged his tail, and chased after him.

"I'm so tricky," Popo shouted as he ran to his group, giggling with delight. Baashir was not amused but he looked at Atafa who gave him a stern look of, "Don't you dare interfere with my gift." Baashir then calmed down, honoring Atafa's wisdom.

CHAPTER SEVEN: HE IS MERCIFUL

All the volunteers will never forget Popo's spirit for life. They will also cherish the kindness from an elderly woman who taught all in the group that day that justice cannot rob mercy. They learned that the Spirit of Christ is the spirit of second chances.

Popo receives a food box from New Hope Ministry in Pakistan

The In-Between— Second Chances

POPO REPRESENTS THOSE WE COME INTO CONTACT WITH ON A DAILY basis. Others may cut in front of our car on the freeway, cut in line at the grocery store, or even win the race to the pulpit on testimony Sunday. It could be something more serious like offending our families, beliefs, or efforts. We have all been offended before and understand what sets us off, so to speak. How do we react? We can choose to uphold justice, mercy, or both.

It is common to focus on the actions of others while ignoring our own action or inaction. The hero of the story was not Popo. He was the learning tool. The hero was not only Atafa, the older woman. Although what she did was an amazing gift, other heroes include the volunteers and also Baashir. He was the one who learned the most in this situation. He was upset at first when Popo didn't observe the rules. But Baashir chose to calm down and learn how to forgive and move on. We can relate to Baashir and hopefully learn that we are all sinners who seek mercy and forgiveness.

We can rejoice and be comforted knowing that we serve a God of second chances. He is a merciful God and allows His children many chances to learn, repent, grow, and improve. None of us would be saved without His mercy nor without the Atonement of Jesus Christ. Every moment of our lives is a second chance.

One popular Bible story of second chances is that of Jonah and the whale. Most kids and adults love this story, but many do not realize the meaning and significance of what Jonah went through before and after entering the whale's mouth.

Before the whale entered the picture, Jonah had tried to run from God's will. He backslid. We often do this when we desire our own will over God's will. Maybe we doubt that God truly knows best by thinking, "No one understands me." Or thinking, "My situation is different," and that we are an exception to what spiritual guidance has been given to everybody else.

God could have let Jonah go his own way, but He loved Jonah too much to let him remain on the wrong path. God loves us so much that He desires to use us, even if that means learning from tough lessons, making us stronger and turning our hearts toward the spirit of truth. Just as each of our trials are individual, God often prepares the perfect lessons for us, and we can choose to learn from them.

Nineveh

The people of the city of Nineveh were distant relatives of the children of Israel. Their common ancestor was the prophet, Noah. For centuries the Ninevites and Israelites had little contact with each other. The Ninevites worshiped the false god Ashur, while the children of Israel worshiped Jehovah, or Jesus Christ.

About 700 BC, God spoke to Jonah, an Israelite prophet, saying, "Arise, go to Nineveh, the great city, and cry against it; for their wickedness is come up before me" (Jonah 1:2). Although Jonah was a prophet and a good man, he was not happy he was asked to do this and "fled from the presence of the Lord" (Jonah 1:10). He ran away from the Lord and headed for Tarshish. Why did Jonah react this way? The Assyrians (Ninevites) were known for their warfare and for being savage brutes. Jonah fled because he feared the Ninevites. I can imagine many of us likely would have responded in the same way Jonah did.

Jonah, wanting nothing to do with the Ninevites, fled in the opposite direction down toward the seaport of Joppa. In Joppa, he found a ship bound for Tarshish, which is likely now present-day Spain (Bible Dictionary, "Tarshish"). After paying the fare, he went aboard the ship, trying to flee from God. Of course, God always knew exactly where Jonah was and what he was trying to get away with. God decided to give Jonah a second chance to prove he feared God more than man (D&C 3:7). The Lord sent a great wind on the sea, and such a violent storm arose that the ship threatened to be broken apart (Jonah 1:4).

The ship's crew began to fear for their lives and the captain was convinced God had sent this wrath due to someone on board. The seamen began to cast lots. When it became clear Jonah was the reason for the danger, the crew asked Jonah, "What shall we do unto thee, that the sea may be calm unto us?" (Jonah 1:11). Jonah now realized that his efforts to hide from the Lord were in vain and replied, "Take me up, and cast me forth into the sea; so shall the sea be calm unto you: for I know that for my sake this great tempest is upon you" (Jonah 1:12).

The crew then threw Jonah overboard to what would have been his certain death. However, as soon as they did this, the seas immediately calmed and a "great fish" sent by the Lord appeared, swallowing Jonah, and thus saving his life (Jonah 1:17). The Lord was merciful, and I think he likely has an amazing sense of humor. I'm not trying to make light of the situation, nor anyone's hardships, but the angels in heaven must have been watching this like a mini-series, wondering what is going to happen next. Can you imagine?

Jonah remained in the whale's belly for three days and three nights. During this time, he humbled himself, acknowledging his sin. From inside the fish, Jonah prayed to the Lord with all his might. He was deep in the realm of the dead when he called for help, and God listened to his cries. Jonah repented and declared, "I am cast out of thy sight; yet I will look again toward thy holy temple" (Jonah 2:4). The engulfing waters threatened him, the deep surrounded him, and seaweed was wrapped around his head. The Lord brought his life up from the pit. But with shouts of grateful praise Jonah vowed to make good. "But I will sacrifice unto thee with the voice of thanksgiving; I will pay that that I have vowed. Salvation is of the Lord. And the Lord spake unto the fish, and it vomited out Jonah upon the dry land" (Jonah 2:9–10).

Then the Lord offered Jonah the chance to follow through with the first command. This time Jonah was determined to set aside his fears of man to ultimately obey the Lord. In the back of his mind he thought God would destroy one of Israel's enemies, the brutal Ninevites! This would be a blessing to his people. This thought gave him even more motivation. He then went forth and preached about God to the people of Nineveh and stayed there for forty days awaiting their destruction. "Yet forty days, and Nineveh shall be overthrown" (Jonah 3:4). After forty days Jonah left and built a shelter so he could watch the grand show as he was sure Ninevah would be torn apart. But, to his disappointment, no destruction came. What happened?

The story continues that the Ninevites actually believed Noah and his preaching, and they began to repent! When Jonah's teachings had reached the king of Nineveh, he and his nobles turned to the Lord. They sent out a decree for a period of fasting, humility, repentance, and prayer throughout the whole city. The Ninevites were joyous for the opportunity to repent. The Lord of second chances also gave the people of Nineveh a second chance, accepting their change of heart and sparing them. The Lord is merciful!

Jonah was disappointed and then complained to the Lord and asked him to take his life, for he felt he was not worth living anymore (Jonah 4:2–3). He once again was focused on his enemies instead of the Lord. He wanted them to be punished for previous sins and couldn't understand how, after all his efforts, the Lord would forgive the Ninevites, who were the enemies of the Israelites.

When Jonah sat to rest, God provided a vine to give him shade. The next day, God sent a worm to eat the vine. Jonah now sat in the hot sun complaining and wanting to die. God called out to Jonah and scolded him for being so concerned and worried about just a plant while God was concerned with the heart condition and lives of 120,000 people who lived in the city of Nineveh (Jonah 4:6–11).

Do Our Enemies Deserve a Second Chance?

There are many of us who can relate to Jonah. Many people I know have sometimes wished for their enemies to be "taught a lesson." We don't want our enemies to have success, but rather to receive the same pain they have seemingly caused for us or for others. "They must know what it is like to be me and suffer as I have." Does this line of thinking sound familiar to you or of someone you know? It can be hard to forgive those who have sinned against us.

I can only imagine how Jonah felt being among his enemies for forty days, preaching goodness, and then the Ninevites quickly repenting and finding favor with the Lord. He likely felt betrayed and then later felt guilty for feeling this way and also for not softening his heart towards their repentance. It can be hard when viewing others as "getting off easy." However, we must trust in the Lord and trust that

He sees the bigger picture. We don't know the hearts of others nor the torment they often suffer in silence. The Ninevites had likely waited a long time to earn a second chance. Their guilt throughout the years must have been agonizing.

Throughout the story of Jonah, we can see where God is merciful and offers second chances. He loves us and wants us to succeed. All of us. "Remember the worth of souls is great in the sight of God" (D&C 18:10). Second chances are also offered to you. However, we must not mistake this mercy as an excuse to continually repeat sin. President Faust has said, "Many of us backslide, many stumble, and I believe firmly in the gospel of the second chance. But the gospel of the second chance means that having once been found weak, . . . thereafter we become steadfast."[1]

When Popo was granted a second chance in the Pakistan food line, those following the rules seemed "punished" for being kind. However, God saw the bigger picture, and Atafa was granted the opportunity to teach all patrons a spiritual lesson in mercy. The opportunity to show compassion outweighed the consequences of hungry bellies. Atafa taught kindness. She taught sacrifice. She taught forgiveness. She taught mercy. She taught second chances.

When the Ninevites were granted mercy, Jonah felt betrayed and let down. However, God saw the bigger picture. He granted Jonah mercy even after Jonah demonstrated he feared man more than he feared the Lord. Jonah was also granted an opportunity to witness a miracle in the mouth of a whale! While inside the whale's mouth, the Lord taught him about repentance. When Jonah was depressed the Ninevites weren't destroyed, the Lord taught him about forgiveness. When God destroyed the vine that was giving Jonah shade, He was teaching him to put more focus on the "condition of the heart" rather than focus on his own physical discomfort. He was also teaching that He is in control of all earthly things.

---

1. James E. Faust, "Stand Up and Be Counted," *Ensign*, Feb. 1982.

CHAPTER SEVEN: HE IS MERCIFUL

The Lord Is on Your Side

If someone has sinned against you, know that God is very mindful of you. Mercy will not rob justice. Put your trust in the Lord that He offers lessons to us all. He is in control of who is offered what lesson in life, and in what way. That is not up to us. We may never know the hardships of our enemies. We may never know of the repentant hearts of those who have sinned against us. We may never know why someone's life "seems to be" so much better than ours. Trust that the Lord is on your side and understands your heartache and thirst for justice. However, He also hears the world's prayers and thirst for His mercy. They are also children of God, and He loves them dearly just as He loves you dearly. He answers each of our prayers individually. He helps us through life lessons individually. He knows our hearts individually. But He offers second chances to all.

Chapter Eight

He Will Guide Us to Safety

....

You Will Be Found

"It's time to go. Get into the car," Dad yelled to the kids. "One, two, three . . . Um, we're missing one." The child who did not get into the car was the main kid who needed to be there. He had a soccer game that afternoon and we had planned on leaving a little early to run a few errands along the way. We then hear the "Clomp! Clomp! Clomp" of someone rushing up the stairs. It was my son, Andrew, who appeared to be in a panic. He came to us with wide eyes, desperately calling for help. "I can't find my cleats!" Dagnabit! We couldn't be overly upset because he was so young, but we knew the plan to run errands before the game was now on the back-burner. The black cleats had to be here somewhere.

"Where did you last wear them?" I asked. He looked at me with a confused look on his face as if to say, "If I knew that then my cleats wouldn't be lost now, would they?" Thus began our search. "Everyone out of the car!" called Dean. The kids begrudgingly hopped out of the car to help find Andrew's shoes. The basement was our first focus. "Look in the playroom, the TV room, and all over Andrew's room," I suggested. Pillows were thrown off couches, we then looked under the cushions. We opened closet doors to scour the belongings. We looked under furniture, behind dressers, and inside the entertainment center. We felt we looked everywhere.

Dean called everyone together in the living room. "Guys, I think we need to pray that Andrew can find his shoes." With that request we hesitantly folded our arms, knowing the kids were now so anxious they couldn't concentrate. Dean then offered a sweet and hopeful prayer, "Heavenly Father, please guide us to Andrew's cleats. This game is very important to him. We have faith he will be able to find them. Amen." No sooner than the "amen" was offered, Andrew perked up and ran outside the back door. Everyone ran out there and began to help him look, thinking he was inspired. After a while of looking everywhere, still nothing. We were confused. Didn't Heavenly Father want our kids to know He answers their prayers? I was frustrated and didn't want this to backfire on us as parents trying to teach our children about faith.

Just then Andrew came running to us with tears in his eyes, "They were under the trampoline mat!" he exclaimed, running towards us with his black cleats in his hands. We had an inground trampoline and it wasn't too unusual to have something fall through the springs. Andrew was so brave and had crawled down underneath the mat and then back up to the grass again. Upon seeing them, he cried tears of joy because he knew God had answered his prayer. It was an amazing lesson to learn that we need to have faith in the Lord *and* must put forth personal effort. We couldn't expect that God was going to make it easy and have the shoes simply appear before us.

Andrew's testimony grew that day. All of the family witnessed what can happen when we put some thought, faith, prayer, and effort into a difficult situation. We still talk about this experience decades later as a testament of inspiration and following the Spirit.

CHAPTER EIGHT: HE WILL GUIDE US TO SAFETY

Finding his lost cleats reminds me of how lost things become found through the Savior and our Heavenly Father. If a nine-year-old's pair of cleats matters, your heart and testimony matter even more.

Lost Keys

If you had five keys on your key ring, and you lost one key, you would be upset. But, why? Wouldn't you just be satisfied you have four other keys? No. You are upset because that key has a specific purpose only it can perform. The other keys cannot open the door that the special key can open. In fact, that key opens the door to your house. Imagine you were away and just arrived home when you found out the key was missing. You really need to get into your house. You would look everywhere for that key and wouldn't give up until you found it. Likewise, you have a specific purpose on this earth that only you were meant to perform. This purpose could range from being an example of righteousness for others to learn from, or could even be to perform a work that is very significant to bring the world His gospel and message of peace. Whatever your purpose is, Heavenly Father values you as His child. He doesn't want to lose you.

Let's up the stakes a little bit. Let's say you lost your cell phone. If you are prepared, you likely have "find my iPhone" on your iPad or something like that. When I misplace my phone, I always ask someone else to call me so I can listen for the ring tone. If I can hear my phone's personal ring, I know I can find it. I am familiar with my ringtone and can tell it apart from other people's ringtones.

Heavenly Father is listening for your "ringtone," or in other words, listening for your personal plea through your prayers. We often keep our cell phones close to us because it is very valuable and important to us. We are even more valuable to Heavenly Father than any cell phone will ever be. He knows our individual prayers and how much they matter. He will not let us stay lost in the gospel but won't force us to stay, either. He will offer every opportunity for us to find Him and live according to His will. If you want to be found, His arms are always open. He loves you so much that He is willing to sacrifice everything for you.

The In-Between— Don't Let Christ's Atonement Be in Vain

THINK OF SOMEONE YOU LOVE WITH ALL YOUR HEART. MAYBE IT IS A spouse, child, parent, sibling, or other relative or friend. You love them so much and don't want any harm to come to them. You don't want to lose them and are very protective of them. Now imagine what would happen if you lost the opportunity to have them in your life. How would that make your heart feel? Heavy? Depressed? Anxious? Now think of Heavenly Father. He loves you so much. But He also loves Jehovah. He loves Jehovah so much too. However, God, the Father, loves you in such a perfect way that He sacrificed His only Begotten Son, the great Jehovah for *you*. He was willing to let Him not only die but suffer on the cross so that *you* could have the ability to repent and return to the fold. This caused Him joy and pain.

It has been suggested God withdrew His spirit while Christ hung on the cross.

> *As a divine being Christ could not fully experience humanity unless he also experienced spiritual death. All humanity are spiritually dead, or "cut off from the presence of the Lord" (Helaman 14:16). I propose that the Spirit could not objectively give Christ the experience of knowing spiritual death, by its very definition, which is to be without the Spirit of God. That could only be understood through the subjective experience—to actually have the Spirit forsake him, to suffer in both body and soul the effects of separation. The separation from the Spirit allowed the condescension of the Son of God to be complete.*[1]

Our Father in Heaven sacrificed so much for us. He allowed the Crucifixion to happen so that we can return to our Father in Heaven again. We cannot let Christ's Atonement be in vain. We matter to God. He has not given up on you. Likewise, He has not given up on a little boy who is simply looking for his cleats. Lost things or even people, can be found.

---

1. Craig Ostler, *The Apostle Paul, His Life and His Testimony: The 23rd Annual Sidney B. Sperry Symposium* (Salt Lake City: Deseret Book, 1994), 159.

CHAPTER EIGHT: HE WILL GUIDE US TO SAFETY

The Lost Sheep

Jesus seems to have shared the parable of the shepherd and the lost sheep more than once. We learn about the parable of the Shepherd and the Lost Sheep in both Mark 18 and in Luke 15. Jesus used the same parable twice. It must be quite important. Since He is the Shepherd and we are considered His sheep, that means we are important.

While the cast of characters (sheep and Shepherd) is the same in both verses, Jesus is talking to two different audiences. In Matthew the parable is given in response to a question asked by Jesus's disciples about who is the greatest. He uses the parable to address appropriate attitudes among His followers.

In Luke 15, the lost sheep parable is given in response to the disapproving comments of religious leaders. This time, He addresses judgmental attitudes toward the "unrighteous" liars and cheaters in the crowd displaying that every person is important to God.

It is from these verses and their passages that we understand it is Jesus who leaves the 99.

Matthew 18:12
How think ye? if a man have an hundred sheep, and one of them be gone astray, doth he not leave the ninety and nine, and goeth into the mountains, and seeketh that which is gone astray?

Luke 15:4
What man of you, having an hundred sheep, if he lose one of them, doth not leave the ninety and nine in the wilderness, and go after that which is lost, until he find it?

One day, some of Jesus's followers began discussing which people were the most important in the kingdom of God. Who is the greatest in the kingdom of heaven? Were kings and queens the most important? Bishops or high priests? Maybe it was the most righteous saints. They must be the most important to God. So, they asked Jesus, "Who is the greatest in the kingdom?" Jesus didn't answer in the way they had expected because to Jesus every person is important in the kingdom of God. Even the smallest child to the greatest sinner, he wants everyone to repent and follow him. Jesus then decided to tell them a parable about the lost sheep.

To understand this story, we need to understand the role of the shepherd. Shepherds love their sheep and even sometimes have names for them. The shepherd leads his sheep to grass to eat, looks for clean water so they can have a drink when thirsty, and makes sure they are safe. He watches after every sheep and takes tender care of them. Sometimes a sheep would fall down a crevice and the shepherd had to climb down and pull it to safety. It would have been common for a shepherd to carry a sheep over their shoulders (Luke 15:5). Unfortunately, there are dangerous animals that would come and try to hurt his sheep. The shepherd protects the sheep and chases all the dangerous animals away so they cannot harm them.

Sometimes the sheep wander off from the rest of the herd and the shepherd calls out the sheep's names. When the sheep hears their name called by the shepherd, they run back to the herd.

Enter the story of the lost sheep: Once a shepherd had one hundred sheep. Every night the shepherd would count his one hundred sheep to make sure they were all there. One day the shepherd counted his sheep and discovered there were only ninety-nine sheep instead of one hundred. The other sheep were safe, but the shepherd was so concerned about the one sheep that was lost that he immediately left the other sheep in a safe place and set off looking for his lost sheep.

Some may feel he should forget about the one he has lost and focus on the other sheep who are already safe in his care. They might suggest, "He should never forget about the ninety-nine to go after the one." What do you think? Should the Shepherd forget about the one? Does it mean he forgets about the ninety-nine if he rescues the one?

The answer is that he doesn't forget the one nor does he forget the ninety-nine. He makes sure the others are safe before going after the one. Every sheep is valuable to him. He is their protector. Likewise, Heavenly Father is your protector. He wants all sheep, meaning us, to enter his fold so you too can feel protected from the evils of the world.

CHAPTER EIGHT: HE WILL GUIDE US TO SAFETY

Come unto the Fold

I used to interpret "fold" to mean a grouping of sheep or animals that belonged to a certain shepherd. I thought "fold" was merely a word describing sheep and that meant we would be a group following God. A fold still relates to sheep, but is so much more.

Elder Randy D. Funk provided this clarification at the April 2022 General Conference:

> *A fold, or sheepfold, is a large enclosure, often constructed with stone walls, where sheep are protected at night. It has only one opening. At the end of the day, the shepherd calls the sheep. They know his voice, and through the gate they enter the safety of the fold. . . . The safety and well-being of the sheep depend on their willingness to come into the fold and to stay in the fold.*[2]

Unfortunately, it seems to have become a trend lately to leave the fold, meaning to not follow Christ. Many previous members of the Church that were once faithful believers now think it is okay to speak poorly of leaders, prophets, and teachings. They have chosen to not only leave the Church, but to leave the fold. This means they have chosen to leave the safety that the commandments, the Word of Wisdom, and the gospel of Jesus Christ has to offer.

Even more unfortunately, there are many who think it is okay to bully other Church members who choose to remain faithful in the gospel of Jesus Christ. These bullies are those who are "lost" in the world, having fallen ill to the philosophies of men. They seem to give more credence to Reddit, a TikTok video, or a Facebook post, than they do the inspired scriptures of the Bible and Book of Mormon—and they make sure everyone knows it. Does this sound familiar?

It is heartbreaking if members in your own family fall into this category of "faith shamers." They, however, are some of the lost sheep talked about in the scriptures. They once belonged to the fold and have now wandered off. They appear to fear the world's judgment more than they fear God's judgment. They know they are not safe

---

2. Randy D. Funk, "Come into the Fold of God," *Ensign*, May 2022, 119.

outside of the fold but may be too stubborn, embarrassed, angry, or scared to return on their own.

However shocking it may be, the Shepherd still wants these rebellious sheep in His kingdom. He wants them back in His safe keeping. He knows they will stop trying to mislead His other sheep once they are back safely into the fold *and* feel seen, heard, forgiven, and accepted. We know the endgame and that even non-believers, including antagonists, will be given a second chance to change their hearts by accessing the Atonement. The Shepherd will find them, "and there shall be one fold and one shepherd; and he shall feed his sheep and in him they shall find pasture" (1 Nephi 22:25).

Another category of sheep are those who want to believe but have doubt or fear because they think they have no place to fit in or are not accepted in our congregations. They may say they don't believe in the gospel but there is a part of them who wants to belong and wants to believe. They want acceptance but don't know if we can offer what they are looking for.

In our high-tech, low-spirituality world, it is easy for others to stray from the fold, always intending to catch up to the Shepherd . . . later. When "later" comes, the world has already convinced them they don't belong in the gospel, even though they do want to belong. In Mosiah we read about those who are "desirous to come into the fold of God, and to be called his people" but need to be kindly led to the fold (Mosiah 18:8). These brothers and sisters may belong to the LGBTQ+ communities, are illegal immigrants, substance abusers, sinners, etc. and may feel like they don't fit in or are too different looking or acting than those who are in the congregation. They may feel alone and believe there is no way back. They often believe the Shepherd has not even noticed they were missing, and no one is looking for them.

These sheep often wander closely to the fold, or even teeter on the edge just waiting for someone to reach out, and keep wandering until someone finds them. If someone other than a Shepherd finds them first, they could be led astray and even further away from the fold. That is why it is so crucial to be diligent in praying and searching for opportunities to be a representative of Christ. Reach out to those who seem to be on your mind. Follow your heart and be open to the Spirit. Invite the sheep back into the fold where they can be

CHAPTER EIGHT: HE WILL GUIDE US TO SAFETY

safe with the flock and the Shepherd. Pick them up, put them on your shoulders, and bring them back to safety. They may say *No* to your invitation, but let them know the fold is always welcoming to them. The Shepherd in the parables isn't worried what the sheep will think of him because he is late. He was more concerned about finding the lost lamb and bringing it home.

There is a third category of sheep. These are people who have yet to hear or accept the gospel. The world is full of hearts waiting to hear about messages of joy and peace. "Other sheep I have which are not of this fold; them also I must bring, and they shall hear my voice; and there shall be one fold, and one shepherd" (3 Nephi 15:17). The world is looking for a Savior. They need Him. They need hope. They desire to feel safe in His fold. Whether we serve proselyting missions, service missions, senior missions, or in any other form of serving in the gospel, we represent the Shepherd who is calling out names to come enter the fold.

The fourth type of sheep are those who are already safely in the fold. They often do their best, mistakes are allowed, and repentance is practiced daily. The fold has become their home.

I love the idea of being brought into the Lord's fold as a group united. It is comforting to know the fold is a place of refuge, safety, and connection, with walls around us to protect us from the harms of the world. However, these sheep need to be willing to share space for the lost sheep the Shepherd brings back into the fold. That is the way of the Shepherd.

I can picture the Savior standing watch over the small opening that might put us in harm's way. Being one-fold with the Savior isn't only about being one in beliefs and understanding, it is about being united within His watch, within His walls of safety and protection.

Elder Funk shares that as the sheep are led through the small opening of the fold, it gives a chance for the shepherd to examine each of them for wounds, to assess their mobility and health, and for him to count each one of them. What a beautiful image for how the Savior watches over each of us as we make the choice to follow Him and enter His fold.[3]

---

3. Randy D. Funk, "Come into the Fold of God," *Ensign*, May 2022, 119.

Stay strong. Heavenly Father has got your back. The Atonement brings comfort knowing that the Savior has walked this same path, even while having loved ones turn against Him. Allow Him to guide you on your journey of being constantly faithful, nothing wavering, and proudly representing The Church of Jesus Christ of Latter-day Saints. Regarding loved ones who are currently "lost sheep"—Heavenly Father will not give up on them and will continue to serve up learning opportunities and chances to live righteously. Keep faith, hope, and an eye single to His glory. Feel comfort knowing the lost sheep will be found.

Chapter Nine

He Accepts Us as We Are

....

Marta the Mighty

THE SINGING RAIN POURED ONTO THE METAL ROOFTOPS, SOUNDING like a percussion band of various symbols throughout the town. Each drop from the skies above arrived with a bang and a clash while the group stared at each other, eyes wide open, waiting to be led to shelter. The teenagers, along with a few adults, huddled underneath two sheets of corrugated metal representing a roof of a house with no walls. "This *is* the shelter," Phil exclaimed to the humanitarians who had arrived in Guatemala just a few days prior. His face shared a huge smile as they all chuckled nervously in unison to show they understood and were grateful for the miniscule umbrella that so many others called their home.

The native faces didn't seem phased by the storm that arrived daily, only lasting for about twenty to thirty minutes at a time. They were used to bringing in their threads and looms to the driest spot they could find. As the rain lifted, the sun peaked out from behind a cloud and the birds chirped once again. The green trees on the mountainside glistened as the light reflected the water dimpled leaves from their branches. The roads were lined with beautifully colored cobblestone the townsfolk had built themselves just five years prior. For a remote jungle town, there was seemingly little garbage in the streets. The larger government did nothing in regard to trash disposal for them. The townsfolk themselves decided to clean up their own community and take honor in their surroundings by uniting together and everyone doing their part. This meant everyone picks up after themselves, cleans the streets, and burns their own garbage.

While people began to once again spread out from under the makeshift roof, Marta continued to demonstrate how she makes bags, sweaters, baby clothing, and even tablecloths using her tools, mainly a small loom. Her sleek, black hair was twisted up into a bun held together by two sticks. She wore a dress of many colors, along with a belt made of braided thread. Her toes were free as she didn't mind walking everywhere in bare feet. I wondered if she couldn't afford shoes and thought it would be a kind gesture to offer her a pair of flip flops I had recently purchased. I reached into my bag and gave them to her. Her confused look told me I may have overstepped my bounds. "She has shoes. Well, sandals. She prefers to go barefoot in her home to show cleanliness and respect," Phil explained while also giving me a glare that said, "Foolish American always thinking you are better than others." Okay, he didn't actually glare and say that. However, I did have an impression from the Spirit that witnessed to me that although I wanted to offer something, maybe I was there in this moment to learn something instead, and to just "be still."

While the group was beckoned to enter the bus to travel to our next stop, Marta called me over to her. Phil came to translate while she handed me a small handbag she had made using her threads and small loom. I shook my head back and forth saying in my beginner Spanish, "No gracias. Quedate con esto y vendeselo a alguien." (No, thank you. You keep this and sell it to someone.) Then, it occurred to me I should offer money and buy it from her. I reached into my backpack to pull out some quetzales while Phil once again glared at me with wide eyes.

CHAPTER NINE: HE ACCEPTS US AS WE ARE

Maybe I didn't offer enough quetzales so I pulled out more bills. Marta had a gentle smile and replied, "Gracias. Sin embargo, este es mi relgalo para ti, por pagar la matricula de Blanca este ano." (Thank you. However, this is my gift to you for paying Blanca's tuition this year).

Before you think I am such an altruistic person, I need to clarify. The truth is we held a fundraiser at one of my schools and the good students in the community donated money to pay for Blanca, Marta's daughter, to go to school and become a secretary. Phil told us the education, and eventual job, will raise her entire family out of severe poverty.

I thanked Marta for the kind gesture and then walked off to get onto the bus. Once we were all seated on the bus awaiting the next stop, Phil leaned over to me and revealed, "Marta has a job farming full time and only makes bags on the side. This bag she gave you likely took her over a month to create." I felt humbled at the kindness Marta showed me. She was a hardworking mother. I had previously felt like I was the one who had so much to offer and that paying the tuition was being such a shining example of the Savior. However, my part was easy. I merely sat at a table in the school selling bracelets. I had relied on others to donate to raise the tuition. Marta was the one teaching me how to be more like the Savior; being humble, and giving of your talents, however big or small.

The In-Between— Sacrifices

MARTA WAS LIKE THE WIDOW IN THE NEW TESTAMENT WHO GAVE OF all she could spare. Marta didn't have much to offer in the way of money or goods, but had collected threads to create a beautiful handbag. She used her talents to offer a gift of thanks. Marta didn't have material wealth just like the widow didn't have material wealth, but rather had a spiritual gift to understand true sacrifice. Her sacrifice was offering all she had. We are to be like Marta and also like the widow. This is more than just us paying tithing, but means to offer all we have to the Lord. The widow's mite is one of those Bible lessons that appear simple on the surface but has layers of meaning for us to unwrap. Let's dig a little deeper.

The Widow's Mite

According to the gospel accounts, Jesus was sitting in the temple near the collection box. Many people came and dropped their offerings into the box. Those who were rich put in large amounts, but this poor woman whose husband had died only had two mites. "The mite, also known as a lepton, was a Jewish coin and the smallest used in New Testament time. At the time of Mark's writing, it was worth 1/64 of a denarius. A denarius was a day's wage for a common worker. In today's terms, it would be worth about 1/8 of a cent."[4]

Jesus commented to His disciples that the widow had put in more than the other people. The majority had put in out of their excess, but the widow had given all that she had.

Mark 12:42–44 (NIV)
But a poor widow came and put in two very small copper coins, worth only a few cents.

Calling his disciples to him, Jesus said, "Truly I tell you, this poor widow has put more into the treasury than all the others.

They all gave out of their wealth; but she, out of her poverty, put in everything—all she had to live on."

Luke 21:1–4 (ESV)
Jesus looked up and saw the rich putting their gifts into the offering box.

And he saw a poor widow put in two small copper coins.

And he said, "Truly, I tell you, this poor widow has put in more than all of them.

For they contributed out of their abundance, but she out of her poverty put in all she had to live on."

---

4. Jennifer Taylor, "The Widow's Mite," *Samford University: University Library*, Jul. 2005, library.samford.edu/special/treasures/2005/mite.html.

CHAPTER NINE: HE ACCEPTS US AS WE ARE

Before we continue to unpack the story of the widow's mite, let's look at the surrounding context of the verse. In Mark 12 the chapter begins with the parable of the tenants. Jesus spoke about a landowner who had a beloved vineyard which he had leased to vinedressers. When the time of the harvest came, the vinedressers treated his servants poorly. So, the man decides to send his son to speak with them, thinking he will get greater respect from the vinedressers, but they kill him instead.

The scribes and Pharisees realized that Jesus had told the parable against them. They were offended and wanted to arrest Him. They couldn't do anything at that time because they feared the people. They left Him alone, but they did not give up. They needed to find a way to turn the people against him, so "they send unto him certain of the Pharisees and of the Herodians, to catch him in his words" (Mark 12:13).

The question the Pharisees and Herodians asked was about paying taxes to Caesar. Jesus responded by telling them to give Caesar what was Caesar's and to give God what belonged to Him. They couldn't dispute that answer but still didn't seem satisfied (Mark 12:16–17). They continued to ask Him more questions, but they couldn't rile nor catch Him in a contradiction. Finally, Jesus told the people to beware of the scribes.

Mark 12:38–40

And he said unto them in his doctrine, Beware of the scribes, which love to go in long clothing, and love salutations in the marketplaces,

And the chief seats in the synagogues, and the uppermost rooms at feasts:

Which devour widows' houses, and for a pretence make long prayers: these shall receive greater damnation.

It's quite interesting that just after this conversation the widow then enters the temple. She puts two coins, or mites, into the collection box. Mites were not worth much, but in comparison to the others who had given before her, the poor widow had given everything.

The Pharisees and Sadducees were so focused on following the letter of the law, they often missed the spirit of the law. Their hearts were upon worldly things, and they didn't follow God's heart. They thought their exact interpretation of laws should be agreed on by everyone, but they didn't consider to first consult God about it.

I'm sure if the Pharisees and Sadducees were to approach the collection box with Jesus watching, they would have put in the exact amount they owed. But that is the problem. They wanted to appear to follow the law more than being kind and understanding. They didn't seem to understand equity. Equity doesn't mean everyone gets nor gives exactly the same amount (or in the same way), but equity means everyone gives (or receives) according to their ability and needs.

The poor widow understood sacrifice. She loved God enough to give Him of all she had. Her heart was in the right place. She didn't have a credit card to fall back on nor money in the bank. She didn't have rich relatives to provide for her needs. Her sacrifice likely meant there would be no food for that day unless there was a miracle. She gave not because she could, but because she wanted to. She was financially broke, but her heart was full of hope. She had faith that the Lord would provide for her needs.

Matthew 6:25, 33

Therefore I say unto you, Take no thought for your life, what ye shall eat, or what ye shall drink; nor yet for your body, what ye shall put on. Is not the life more than meat, and the body than raiment?

But seek ye first the kingdom of God, and his righteousness; and all these things shall be added unto you.

CHAPTER NINE: HE ACCEPTS US AS WE ARE

The Bigger Picture

What can we learn from the widow and also from Marta? As members of The Church of Jesus Christ of Latter-day Saints we have been called as representatives of Christ. We should not think we are better than others nor have more to offer merely because we are monetarily wealthy, more educated, own a nice house, or wear stylish clothing. We have been set apart for the purpose of sharing the light of Christ with others. As followers of Christ, we are called upon to make our lives a living sacrifice to Heavenly Father who sent His Son to die for us. This could mean sacrificing monetarily or even sharing of our talents to help lighten others' burdens.

Some may donate money, some donate time, some donate skills they have developed ranging from construction, art, photography, beautification, singing, writing, serving in a calling, or giving of your time and offering a listening ear. The possibilities are endless of what may be a sacrificial offering for you to share and help build up the kingdom of God.

Marta gave of her talents, materials, and efforts. She didn't let her family go bankrupt over the issue. She still used discernment and created a plan. She planned her time for the month, along with her budget, and created a handbag for me. This taught me that sacrifice doesn't always mean you give up everything you own nor that you risk losing your own life. Some have argued that the widow shouldn't have given two mites and risked starving to death. I think we need to give her more credit than some do. I think she had so much faith that Heavenly Father would take care of her, she knew she could offer the two mites and she would still survive. We are not asked to be the Savior and sacrifice our lives as He sacrificed His. However, we are asked to be like the Savior when He gave of His time, talents, and efforts.

I will admit I used to struggle with tithing. I didn't struggle when we were first married and made little income, meaning our tithing was two to three hundred dollars at most, during a good month. I did struggle as our income increased and that meant our tithing increased as well. I had to study and understand what the scripture about the rich man versus the poor man entering the kingdom of God meant to me personally. "Then said Jesus unto his disciples, Verily I say unto you, That a rich man shall hardly enter into the kingdom of heaven. And again I say unto you, It is easier for a camel to go through the eye of a needle, than for a rich man to enter into the kingdom of God" (Matthew 19:23–24).

When it comes to sacrifice for the Lord, I don't think the scripture in Matthew is only talking about money. It is also talking about abundance of time, talents, efforts, attitudes, and abilities. Are we more like the rich man's heart or more like the poor man's heart? I have been guilty of the former. Why is it so hard to give of abundance? I believe it is because we feel we have earned "it" and deserve "it." "It" can represent money, time, vacations, toys, large homes, large yards, and other comforts. We will always have a list of extra comforts of the latest and greatest trends we wish to obtain. We have owned our share of boats, ATVs, campers, and other extras. We have created some very fun family memories on the lake, in the mountains, or at the beach. I am thankful for those opportunities. However, our favorite memories have been when we needed to be creative and extend a little more effort, without using monetary resources.

One spring break we asked our kids what they wanted to do. Generally we would have gone on a cruise to a tropical location, flown to a beach house, and done something super relaxing and what we would justify as "self-care." To our surprise our girls had decided they wanted to go on a temple tour throughout Utah doing baptisms. At first I was a bit disappointed and didn't really want to take a long road trip, but my mama heart felt proud that these young women were guided by the Spirit to use their vacation time to serve the Lord. We teamed up with another family and started in the northern part of the state and ended up in St. George, visiting temples along the way. Some did baptisms and confirmations while others did initiatory work.

We had a fun time staying at bed and breakfasts along the way and enjoyed each other's company. We didn't give of "all we had," but we sacrificed of our time and efforts. It was a unique way to offer our mites to our Father in Heaven. Although the girls in our party have gone different directions, I know that when the time is right, their hearts will remember the bond we created and the Spirit they felt in the temple. It was truly a blessed time to serve the Lord together.

CHAPTER NINE: HE ACCEPTS US AS WE ARE

Your Mites

Some people think they don't have much to offer and they often don't recognize their talents. It can be easy to sit at the back of the room and never really contribute so much as a comment. Many people have really good excuses to choose out of activities, relationships, and opportunities. Maybe we are mentally and physically exhausted and it is all we can do to just make it to the chapel. However, I know for me, there are many weeks I can offer more than I have.

Your "widow's mite" may mean helping a neighbor, extending an arm of friendship, setting up chairs in the primary room, or clearing snow from walkways at the church. Whatever your sacrifice is, Heavenly Father knows your abilities. He knows if you are burying your talents or instead seeking to help build up the kingdom of God. He doesn't ask that you sacrifice your life nor sacrifice your family relationships. He just asks that you show up willing to be led by the Spirit to meet the need of those you come in contact with.

Just as God answers prayers individually, He is mindful of our individual situations. Jesus saw the poor widow's sacrifice and He is mindful of your sacrifices as well. He is more in tune with the state of our hearts and offerings than the amount of those offerings. God knows that when our hearts are in the right place, everything else will fall into place as well.

Chapter Ten

He Celebrates Diversity

....

Cookie Cutters

THE STUDENTS SAT ON STURDY BROWN CHAIRS ARRANGED IN A circle, all wearing royal blue shirts that said, "Escuela de Tecnologia Moderna." The room was surrounded by windows opening to the Ceiba trees and fuchsia pink Hedychium plants which shared their shade and beauty with all onlookers. The noise from the air conditioning was consistent and meditating; meaning, the high ceiling fan that slowly turned and made a "rooum" sound with each rotation. It was muggy but bearable in the early morning hours. The clean smell of early rain was refreshing and welcoming.

It was the day the humanitarian workers were to teach the Guatemalans how to interact with gringos. The goal was to teach them social skills so they could work in Guatemala City in a hotel or other customer service area. Us "educated" gringos just knew we had the right way of running a business and we were going to teach the kids how Americans appropriately communicate with humans. Or, so our prideful minds thought.

At first, we were frustrated because the teens wouldn't look any of us in the eye. In America, not making eye contact may be seen as disrespectful. In Guatemala it was just the opposite and actually a sign of showing respect. Who is right? Which culture has the better social skills?

My assigned task was to teach them how to appropriately greet someone. I went around the circle and let each student practice shaking my hand and saying, "Hello. My name is _____. How are you?" The students were instructed to look me in the eyes while doing this.

One teen boy was really struggling meeting my eyes. He just couldn't do it. He looked down, looked to the side; he looked anywhere but up to my face. My heart softened and I thought, "What are we doing? This is their culture. Who are we to say our way is better than their way?"

Then the young boy began to giggle. He then looked up at me, very briefly making eye contact, then looking behind me. I then realized the main reason he was struggling looking at me was because his friend was directly behind my head making silly faces at him, trying to mess him up. "Juan? That's enough," directed their teacher. It was pretty funny and soon the entire room began to giggle. It helped to ease all the tension, and everyone soon began to relax. I then shared while someone translated, "It's okay if this is uncomfortable for you. Sometimes it is uncomfortable for me too and I have had years of practice. You can practice this type of introduction if it will help you get a job in the city. If not, it is okay to honor your traditions and we can just practice some English greeting words."

Maybe it was all the giggling or that they weren't being forced to do it, but after we discussed the purpose of the exercise, every single student was able to make eye contact with me without feeling any shame, but rather feeling more confident. We all became instant friends and enjoyed the remaining lessons and activities of the day.

In life we often get in our minds that things should "look a certain way." I call this the "Cookie Cutter" principle. We think everything should have an exact pattern or way and that life should go exactly as planned. When things do not go according to the picture in our minds, we have confusion, anxiety, distress, or even depression. We may think either we or someone else has done something wrong or even sinned. This can cause chaos in our minds. In that school room two different cultures were uniting and discovering different ways of communicating. No one way was better than the other. We were simply willing to learn from each other.

Uniqueness

Picture a small child who has recently had a birthday and received three wrapped presents. They were able to unwrap those presents and find toys that now belong to them. What may happen when they are at another birthday celebration for someone else? They might see the presents and think they are for them as well. Or they may see four presents and wonder why their friend got more presents. They likely have a hard time getting the cookie cutter picture of what all birthdays should look like out of their minds.

The reality is, everyone celebrates birthdays differently. Some get five presents, some get no presents, some buy others presents. There isn't one right way to do it. It is individual.

Christ taught communities, but applies the Atonement individually. The gospel is unifying for everyone, but we each worship individually. Even the customs of our congregations vary throughout the world, although gospel principles remain constant.

I remember going to church in Hawaii when I was in high school, and being confused that their sacrament trays were round when ours at home were rectangular. Recently, someone in our congregation made a 3-D copy of the bread tray providing individual spots for each small piece of bread. Another tray also provided individual spots for the water cups in order to avoid germs being spread. The first time I saw these trays my heart sank because we had to take such precautions to be safe from viruses. Then, I realized what a blessing it was to have technology to create such an innovative way to offer the sacrament.

When I attended a different sacrament service, they didn't have the fancy trays like we did. However, it didn't make the sacrament any less sacred and valuable. I was still able to renew my covenants regardless of what the trays looked like.

I think Heavenly Father looks at us the same say. Some have fancy lives, some have fancy bodies, some have fancy homes or cars. Others have more humble lives, humble bodies, humble homes or cars. The point is that not everyone has a "Cookie Cutter" life, and that is fantastic. God wants us to be individuals. He wants us each to learn how to use agency appropriately and that means we all have individual lessons to experience and learn from. How boring would life be if we were all exactly the same? I am so thankful for variety, even if that means ups, downs, and all arounds in life.

> *Being unified in Christ doesn't mean we all must be the same. . . . Today, missionaries from The Church of Jesus Christ of Latter-day Saints serve in more than 400 missions worldwide. Church publications are printed in 188 languages. Over 30,000 congregations meet each Sunday in North and South America, Europe, Asia, Africa, and throughout the Pacific.*
>
> *Latter-day scripture teaches us that the diversity of Church members should enhance our united work in preparation for the Lord's Second Coming. This distinctiveness includes racial, ethnic, gender, and language differences, as well as our varied gifts, perspectives, and experiences.*[1]

Galatians 3:28
There is neither Jew nor Gentile, there is neither bond nor free, there is neither male nor female: for ye are all one in Christ Jesus.

1 Corinthians 12:12–14 (NIV)
Just as a body, though one, has many parts, but all its many parts form one body, so it is with Christ.

---

1. Bryant Jensen, "The Blessings of Diversity," *Ensign*, Jul. 2019, https://www.churchofjesuschrist.com.

CHAPTER TEN: HE CELEBRATES DIVERSITY

For we were all baptized by one Spirit so as to form one body—whether Jews or Gentiles, slave or free—and we were all given the one Spirit to drink.

Even so the body is not made up of one part but of many.

Should You Seek to Fit in or Seek to Stand Out?

You have tried to follow the good example of other members. You go to church, take the sacrament, read your scriptures, say your prayers, but you still feel different from everyone else. You look around the congregation and realize no one else has a life like yours. They seem so different. Some appear to have all the luck. Some appear to have all the sorrow. How is that possible? How can one life look so different from another when both people strive to live the gospel and its principles?

Too many of us feel like the odd member out, a forgotten child of God in a world of "cookie-cutter" members. "When we compare ourselves to others, we may feel disappointed—cheated, even—especially if we've been trying to live the standards we've been told will bring us happiness."[2]

Rather than compare ourselves to others, we should celebrate our diversity. The Lord needs our diversity. The church members need our diversity. Those awaiting to hear the gospel need our diversity. Those who have fallen away wondering how to come back, need our diversity. I don't know of any prophet, scripture, or conference talk that has ever stated we had to live a picture perfect lifestyle to be accepted by God. Some think that to be considered a good member they have to be married by the age of twenty-two, graduate from BYU by age 23 (after a mission, of course), own a cute little house with a white picket fence, have multitudes of obedient children, eat food only from their garden, sew their own clothing, do genealogy day and night, and only then they can enter the kingdom of heaven. I know that is an exaggeration. But, the point is there is no scripture saying we are required

---

2. Marian Spencer, "Why Don't I Feel Like a 'Cookie Cutter' Mormon?" *Third Hour*, 5 Apr. 2016, https://thirdhour.org/blog/life/dont-feel-like-fit-gospel/.

to be "cookie cutter," or perfect to be worthy of God's love. We are meant to be individuals who are examples of the million different ways we can live a life leading to Christ.

The In-Between— The Lord Needs Our Diversity

It says the word "welcome" on our church houses. Do we mean it? Do we just talk with our direct neighbors instead of reaching out to those we don't often see? Do we associate with those who are similar to us or instead reach out to others we have nothing in common with other than the gospel? How awesome would it be if you opened your mind, opened your heart, and opened your door to someone who was very different from you? Would that be hard? Maybe. But you have no idea the relationships you miss out on by not reaching out.

In this day and age of technology, which has been so detrimental to physical and social connection, we can also use the same technology as a tool to reach out to others. Send a text, e-mail, use messenger, etc. to let others know you are thinking of them. Meet them where they are in life and not where you think they need to be. If they like sports, go see a game with them. Maybe they like gardening—help them plant some seeds. The point is, get to know them! Don't do this so you can feel better about yourself like you are such a good person (like I originally approached teaching eye contact), but rather as a way to unite as followers of Christ.

There are many with talents that remain hidden because no one takes the time to invite them to share. Yes, it is up to the individual to offer their skills or efforts, but I feel those who already feel comfortable in the gospel should be the ones reaching out to those who may not feel as comfortable. It is a much easier position to be in, so do it!

Who Is Your Neighbor?

We have been admonished to minister to our neighbors. What if your neighbor has tattoos? Gasp! What if they struggle with a few gospel principles? Like that has never happened before (sarcasm). What if

CHAPTER TEN: HE CELEBRATES DIVERSITY

they mow their lawns on a Sunday and then play basketball without their shirts on? Oh, my! I am not trying to make fun of stereotypes of those who many may call "heathens," but the truth is, we are all sinners. We are all doing the best we can, with the knowledge we have gained, and experiences we have learned from. We should not judge others just because they sin differently than we do. We can remain true to gospel principles and be a light to others when the world seems so dark. The seeds of the gospel we plant now will someday be fruitful. It may not be until Christ comes again, but He is the Master Gardener and will know how to reach your neighbor in a way that is in unison with their uniqueness. Because of your friendship, the gospel will sound familiar to them. They will recognize the Spirit and feel the love of the Lord. It will be glorious!

In the concluding days of His mortal ministry, Jesus gave His disciples what He called "a new commandment" (John 13:34). Repeated three times, that commandment was simple but difficult: "Love one another, as I have loved you" (John 15:12; see also verse 17). The teaching to love one another had been a central teaching of the Savior's ministry. The second great commandment was "love thy neighbour as thyself" (Matthew 22:39). Jesus even taught, "Love your enemies" (Matthew 5:44). But the commandment to love others as He does (John 13:35) was to His disciples—and is to us—a challenge that was unique. President Thomas S. Monson taught, "Love is the very essence of the gospel, and Jesus Christ is our Exemplar. His life was a legacy of love."[3]

Elder D. Todd Christofferson of the Quorum of the Twelve Apostles has said:

> *The diversity we find now in the Church may be just the beginning. . . . It's not just diversity for diversity's sake, but the fact that people can bring different gifts and perspectives. And the wide range of experience and backgrounds and challenges that people face will show us what really is essential in the gospel of Christ. And much of the rest that's been, perhaps, acquired over*

---

3. Thomas S. Monson, "Love—the Essence of the Gospel," *Ensign*, May 2014, 91.

time and is more cultural than doctrinal can slip away, and we can really learn to be disciples.[4]

Our differences, in other words, should help us better understand and live the restored gospel of Jesus Christ.

Different and the Same

We are all created in the image of God (Genesis 1:27). Not one of us was made apart from the creative, thoughtful design of our Creator (Psalm 139:13–14). We are all created equally on purpose. God does not discriminate and make one human better than another. We may all have different skin, eyes, body shapes, and other physical traits, yet we are all the same and created to reflect and worship Him, our Father in Heaven. Jesus died for every tribe, tongue, and nation.

If we know we are all children of the same God, why can it seem so difficult to have Christlike love for one another? It can be difficult because we must live among those who do not share our same beliefs, values, and religious practices. Just before His Crucifixion, Jesus prayed for His followers: "I have given them thy word; and the world hath hated them, because they are not of the world, even as I am not of the world" (John 17:14). We are not of this world; we are children of God.

We fought for agency in the premortal existence knowing this may cause torment and disagreements with those we love. We knew it also meant we would make mistakes and have to find our own way back to the covenant path, with bumps and bruises along the way. We also knew this meant our fellow brothers and sisters may make choices not in accordance with the teachings of Jesus Christ. I am sure this broke our hearts. However, we knew the alternative was Satan's plan and was not the plan of our Heavenly Father.

Christ then pleaded to Heavenly Father, "I pray not that thou shouldest take them out of the world, but that thou shouldest keep them from the evil. They are not of the world, even as I am not of

---

4. D. Todd Christofferson, "Is There a Place for Me?" *YouTube*, 21 Oct. 2016, 2:37, https://www.youtube.com/watch?v=SHq1HCiDbCI.

the world (John 17:15–16). He repeated the phrase *"not of this world"* over and over. These words matter. We are to follow Christ and not follow this world. We knew we would stand out and be hated for following Christ. We knew those who once fought alongside us against Satan and his angels would be the very same ones to mock us and call us heretics, racists, homophobes, backwards, old-fashioned, a cult . . . you get the picture.

We knew our brothers and sisters may fall away from the light. What are we directed to do about their actions and mockery of our religious beliefs? We are directed to "love one another," but it goes even deeper than that. I have often heard, "hate the sin, but love the sinner." That is good. However, we are capable of more. Love can be a feeling or a descriptive word, but love must also be an action.

The answer on how to treat our fellow man is found in John 17:21, "That they all may be one; as thou, Father art in me, and I in thee, that they also may be one in us: that the world may believe that thou hast sent me."

Rocking the Boat

How can we become one people if we are constantly mocking or in judgment of one another? We cannot. We can remain firm in our beliefs, never apologizing for the gospel of Jesus Christ, and still be kind. We may have to be okay with not agreeing about everything.

I was recently teaching some elementary students the different personality traits and the difference of being passive, aggressive, and assertive in regard to communication. They loved learning how to control their emotions and still clearly communicate their needs.

To me, *passive membership* in the gospel means you simply do nothing and avoid ever sticking up for your beliefs. You are afraid to rock the boat, so to speak, so you avoid even turning the boat's engine on. This boat never goes anywhere but instead remains in the harbor. You are safe there, but you never experience growth. Your testimony isn't shaken, but it isn't strengthened either.

Being an *aggressive follower* means you likely take offense over anything someone says or does against your beliefs. Maybe you are offended someone didn't minister to you when you needed. Now, for example, you are upset making social media posts discrediting the gospel plan. When we meet chaos with chaos, we aren't putting out a fuse, but rather igniting it. When we argue aggressively it is as if our boat is fighting and pushing other boats out of the harbor. This can cause contention with the other party feeling even stronger about their rhetoric, and your boat of emotions is crashing against the waves! This leads to hurt feelings of both parties and feeling justified about our own "over the top" actions. Although both parties think they each have won a debate, no one wins in this scenario because both hearts are now full of contention. This is not of Christ.

Being an *assertive member* means to be confident, but polite—without the drama. This doesn't mean people should get away with demeaning comments and actions, but does mean you are confident enough in your beliefs, they can't rock your boat. You are the captain and can steer that boat in whichever direction you want.

The Discomfort Zone

The way we view stress or discomfort can determine the outcome of our experiences. You may not believe what I am about to say, but stress is a gift from God. Before your eyes roll to the back of your head, hear me out. Stress has been given to us to help prepare our bodies to take action. The energy created by stress helps us achieve goals, prepares us to run for a touchdown, take care of a crying child, prepare a meal for a neighbor, and even to attend the temple. Stress, in small doses, is healthy!

Think of what your body is doing right now. Are you sitting, standing, laying down? If you are awake right now, and I believe you are, your body requires enough stress to accomplish that task.

The key is in how we view and manage our stress. Too much or too little stress can be detrimental to our bodies and minds. For instance, I work with students who sometimes have panic attacks. I teach them how to calm down their bodies and their minds. Much to their surprise, we can generally accomplish the calming down in less than a minute. Some call me a miracle worker and some think I am a magician. The

CHAPTER TEN: HE CELEBRATES DIVERSITY

key really is to have the knowledge and confidence that we can control our bodies and minds. The students view me as their mentor. The trust we have built creates a bond and they then feel confidence in me and also in themselves. I love these kids, they know it, and they know I will help them. I really do have the best job in the world!

Their anxiety generally begins to take root while in the middle of the discomfort zone. To them, the discomfort zone isn't much fun at all. In fact, it can be really hard to sit in the discomfort zone. They view life like a bullseye. They see one end result and no room for

The discomfort zone leading to the panic zone

growth. They do believe one road leads to another, but goes from comfort to discomfort and ends in panic. In their minds, discomfort can only lead to something negative, meaning everything is predetermined and they feel out of control.

For example, my students change grade levels and teachers every year. This is the discomfort zone for them. It means change from what was familiar. Many students struggle with that change and the new expectations because this also means having to make new friends, finding a new place to hang your backpack, and having a new time to each lunch. Because of this discomfort, some students end up in my office asking for my help. They view discomfort as something bad and try to avoid it at all costs.

However, the students who are the most successful during the school year are those who view discomfort as an opportunity for growth. Once they acknowledge the discomfort zone as a chance to learn a new way to approach situations, they then learn to work through many challenges on their own. These students may view a new teacher as an opportunity to learn different styles of teaching, a new class as a way to meet new people and friends, and see that adjusting to a different lunch time will be okay. These students may still prefer the comfort zone, and may get frustrated in the discomfort zone, but also believe they will figure out a way to learn and grow through the zones. This attitude leads to arrival in the confidence zone. They know they will still have discomfort, but have enough confidence that they can and will work through whatever challenge happens during the school year. This could mean learning from a new math problem, making new friends and expanding your social circle, or even finding something new to do at recess when all the basketballs are taken.

The goal is to be comfortable with discomfort. This leads to feeling confident we can manage the obstacles in life. This confidence leads to the sweet spot. When you are in the sweet spot, you don't overthink a situation. You know life will have its ups and downs, just like a heartbeat, but also know that having a heartbeat means you are alive and can work through whatever trial is thrown your direction.

It comes down to how we view stress. Too little stress means no growth. Too much stress can lead to negative physical affects and a clinical diagnosis of anxiety, depression, or other mental health issue. If you can manage the stress level and channel the energy from that stress, you land in the sweet spot and can create miracles. Listen to your body and ask what the energy is trying to prepare you for. Is your body preparing you for an upcoming test, a difficult decision you must make, working in the yard, serving dinner to your family, or even learning something new? Thank your body for giving you the energy needed to accomplish that task. Then, let it go.

This means release that energy in an appropriate way. If you feel your body having too much energy, there are many ways to help you self-regulate your emotions. Some people go for a walk, create art, play a sport, listen to music, go for a drive, whatever it takes to get their emotions in check. We have been given the gift of discernment to know what our bodies crave.

We have been challenged to begin to see the good, not just in others, but to see the good in ourselves. When we carry heavy burdens, it can be easy to feel overwhelmed and like giving up. The bottom line is you do you. What efforts you feel you can make regarding stress or anxiety, is between you and Lord. Don't underestimate yourself, however, as you were born for greatness. But know, it is okay to protect yourself, your time, and your efforts when needed. Henry B. Eyring stated, "Most people carrying heavy loads begin to doubt themselves and their own worth. We lighten their loads as we are patient with their weaknesses and celebrate whatever goodness we can see in them. The Lord does that."[5]

Just like my students sometimes need a mentor to help them throughout the school day, our personal mentor is the Savior, Jesus Christ. It is a blessing to know He has confidence in each of us that we can and will work through our earthly experiences. Whatever happens. Heavenly Father gave us earthly bodies so we can learn, grow, and gain knowledge on controlling the physical and mental nature of our existence. This is preparing us to become resurrected. This is preparing us to be exalted. This is preparing us to become like Him. He didn't promise it would be easy, but we all knew that it would be worth it.

Italians Can Marry Irish, They Make Beautiful Children

An experience that was very uncomfortable for me but provided an opportunity for growth was when I was looking for my husband's ancestors. My children didn't really know their Italian side and we were one of two families carrying the Porcelli surname in all of Utah.

---

5. Henry B. Eyring, "The Caregiver," *Ensign*, Nov. 2012, 124.

The internet was fairly new and the white pages hadn't started charging yet to look up names and phone numbers. I looked up Porcelli in the New York registry and began calling. The very first phone call went like this:

"Hello, ma'am. This is Michelle Porcelli. I am looking for my husband's relatives. Do you know a Tony Porcelli by chance?"

"Yes, of course I do. That is my husband."

"No, it's not. Tony is my husband."

"You are incorrect. Tony is my husband."

Long story short, my first phone call was unknowingly Dean's Aunt Angie whom he had never met. Her husband really was named Tony. It didn't occur to either of us there could be more than one Tony.

We decided to fly out to New York within the next few weeks to meet her. She was our link to Dean's Italian heritage no one else seemed to know much about. His father had left the family when Dean was quite young, rarely seeing them again, and they didn't have much information about his extended family. Angie was the last of the generation of immigrants and one of our final hopes to do genealogy and get the scoop on this Italian ancestry.

We met her in Westchester County to search for vital records, birth, marriage, and death certificates. I remember the first time I saw her. She stood on the top step of the courthouse, with her four-foot ten-inch frame, white hair glistening in the winter sun, a brown overcoat, and large handbag hanging over one of her shoulders. When she saw my husband, she knew he belonged in their family. "All the Porcelli men were so handsome," she claimed with delight as we walked up to her. "You are larger than an Italian should be, though." I was trying not to laugh while Dean remained silent and gave her a big hug.

The brisk breeze made our cheeks burn and noses run a little, but the sunshine was a welcome delight. Aunt Angie then turned her head to me to get a closer look. Her eyes met mine and then she looked me up and down to case out the situation. Her long pause made me wonder what she was thinking. Others were walking by us going in and out of the building. She waited until no one else was around and declared, "You are obviously not Italian." She paused while I froze in the moment. Then she pursed her lips into a half smiled and asked, "Are you Irish? Italians can marry Irish. They make beautiful

CHAPTER TEN: HE CELEBRATES DIVERSITY

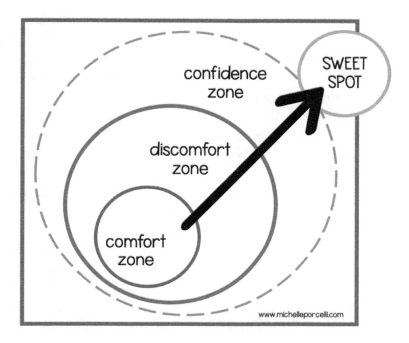

Discomfort zone leading to the sweet spot

children." I didn't know if I should laugh or cry. But squeaked out, "I am Swedish, English, a bit of a melting pot." "Oh," was her only response as she looked a bit disgusted.

I could have chosen to be offended, but that wouldn't accomplish much more than wasted money and time on the trip. We secretly nicknamed her Marie, from the show *Everybody Loves Raymond*, and thought she was simply awesome to speak her mind. We chose to sit in the discomfort and prayed we could learn something from this regarding which direction and action to take next. It was up to us how we would to receive her words and we chose to be in control of any negative emotions. Aunt Angie was just acting as herself and she made for an interesting and fun trip.

Once we all relaxed a bit, we engaged in some family conversation learning more about the Italian side of our family. She told us Dean's father had ran away at the age of thirteen! He was escaping an abusive home and landed in many states across the United States. He came home periodically to New York, but family relationships were always strained. She showed us pictures of aunts and uncles and I saw my children's faces and skin tones among the relatives. I thought Aunt Angie was warming up to us, things seemed to be going well, and we had passed through the discomfort zone. However, in regard to "zones," Dean and I chose different routes at dinner that evening.

At a restaurant, Aunt Angie was confused by some of my choices. "Would you like a beer?" she inquired.

"No thank you. We don't drink beer," I responded, matter-of-factly.

"You don't drink beer? What do you drink then?" she said a bit confused.

"Water. We drink water," I was hoping to not sound annoyed.

"Water? Who drinks water?" she scowled.

I chuckled inside and hoped she wouldn't notice.

Then the question bomb happened. I don't know why the seating ended up this way, but she sat at the head of the table, with cousins we had just met sitting on the sides, and I was at the foot of the table. Oh boy! All the cousins seemed nice, so I wasn't too uncomfortable with them. But, they definitely knew to give Aunt Angie respect when she spoke.

She stood up with her tiny frame and put her hands on the table as she leaned forward. We knew she meant business. She was leaning in my direction and asked, "Are you Catholic?"

I was about to be completely ostracized from the family. "No," I squeaked out.

"No? What are you then?" she sternly questioned. She looked confused and frustrated but was now speechless.

I felt paralyzed, frozen in the moment, not wanting to tell her about my religious beliefs because I didn't know what she had already heard about our religion. People are more inclined to hear negative rumors and ignore the beauty or truth of the gospel. I didn't know what type of "ground" I was on. I had now passed from the discomfort zone to the panic zone.

Thankfully, my husband, who has never apologized for his beliefs, leaned in and assertively announced, "We are Mormon." The cat had finally exited the bag. Not only was I a member of The Church of Jesus Christ of Latter-day Saints, AKA Mormons pre-2018, her precious "newfound" nephew had also been baptized into the Latter-day Saint church and not the Catholic church like his father was. But,

CHAPTER TEN: HE CELEBRATES DIVERSITY

Dean had chosen to pass from discomfort to the confidence zone. Everyone could see he was unapologetically, Mormon.

Everyone at the table was silent, awaiting to see Aunt Angie's response. I'm sure they were either fearful of what her next words would be, or they were excited to see some sort of fireworks show between us. They all knew Dean wasn't "supposed to" marry outside of the Italian heritage and now he had married outside the presiding family religion. Aunt Angie paused for a moment. She looked around. "Hmmm. You know one of your churches is being built right across the street from my apartment? I think I might go take a tour of it." Whew! We were off the hook of negativity. Everyone at the table appeared to relax and casual conversation started up again amongst the cousins.

Dean and I had a decision to make. Every question Aunt Angie had asked us on this trip seemed like an accusation. We could have been very offended, and we were in our right to feel that way. Instead, we chose to embrace the moment and enjoy all of our differences. We then relished every question that followed about our lives and beliefs. Their questions seemed more out of curiosity than accusations. I think that is the blessing of choosing to "not be offended." Your interpretation of words/questions/actions appear more positive than negative. We showed love and confidence in who we are to these newfound relatives.

We explained about the concept that we believe "Families are Forever" and they thought that was pretty cool. Some then looked at each other and wondered if they really wanted to spend eternity with all their children. It was funny to hear they weren't sure if they truly liked that concept or not. What could have been a disaster became a very spiritual and comfortable time at the restaurant.

The Lord repeats the concept of "becoming as one": "And the glory which thou gavest me I have given them; that they may be one, even as we are one" (John 17:22). In verse 26 we learn about sharing God's name or light and what happens when we are not ashamed of our beliefs and become as one: "And I have declared unto them thy name, and will declare it: that the love wherewith thou hast loved me may be in them, and I in them."

Elder Dallin H. Oaks said:

In so many relationships and circumstances in life, we must live with differences. . . . as followers of Christ we should live peacefully with others who do not share our values or accept the teachings upon which they are based. . . . That includes loving our neighbors of different cultures and beliefs as He has loved us. As a Book of Mormon prophet taught, we must press forward, having "a love of God and of all men" (2 Nephi 31:20).[6]

I have not been very grateful for challenges in the moment. That is very hard. But I can look back on experiences God has given me and know that each learning opportunity has been created individually for my testimony. God is mindful of difficulties in relationships. He understands cultural practices and beliefs. He understands wanting to fit the "cookie cutter" mold and wanting to fit in. He also understands that we are capable of breaking that mold to become more; to become a light to the world. Darkness cannot exist where there is light. Don't let your flame blow out due to someone else's intended offense. Hold onto your testimony, be confident, and know you are doing the best you can.

Why fit in when you were born to stand out. —Dr. Seuss

---

6. Dallin H. Oaks, "Loving Others and Living with Differences," *Ensign*, Nov. 2015, 28.

Chapter Eleven

You Will Be Found!

....

No More Missed Chances

A HIGH-PITCHED BELL CHIMES SIGNALING THERE IS A MESSAGE WAITing for me. I read the text that was just sent by a member of our bishopric, "Sister Porcelli, a visitor at the chapel would like to meet you." Oh, heavens! I feel pretty proud of myself knowing this visitor must have been in our sacrament meeting and loved my testimony which I bore that same morning. I was feeling rather special and thought my words must have touched their heart. I thought, "Thank heavens I was there at church so I could have such an impact on this stranger" . . . Not!

Unbeknownst to others, I generally change out of my church clothing as soon as I get home from the services, put on my cozy sweats, along with a soft hoodie. I was too lazy to go to the church to meet this visitor and texted back, "Go ahead and give them my cell number and they can contact me." Then . . . crickets! I didn't hear anything back for about an hour. Finally, another text arrived, "She doesn't have access to a phone and says it's fine." What? What's fine? I then call Brother Keeley to chat with him and see what this is all about. "Well, she was attending the sacrament meeting that met right after our meeting and saw your daughter's missionary plaque hanging up in the hallway. She says that your daughter is one of the missionaries who helped activate her. However, she cannot call you because she is a resident of the treatment center."

My heart sank. Not only did she not hear my testimony . . . ha ha . . . but I knew I had messed up on a chance to speak with someone who my daughter taught on her mission. I let my coziness and pride get in the way of courtesy and kindness. There had indeed been a treatment center in our town. It was a recovery home with around twelve residents and I didn't know much more about it than that. I called to chat with this business to see if they could help me get in contact with the lady who had been reaching out to me.

Unfortunately, upon speaking with me, they said they couldn't tell me if she was a resident there or not, needing to keep confidentiality. This is where my gumption takes over, although I try to not be too overbearing, but I let the Spirit dictate my words, "I already know she is at your treatment facility because she told our ward clerk. Will you please tell her I want her to come to our Relief Society activity on Thursday evening? It is an outdoor picnic and I can pick her up." They agreed to pass along the message, and said "if" she were there, it might be a good idea for her to interact with me and get out for some rejuvenating conversation and support. They also said they would have to accompany her, "if" she were their patient, and they would meet me there. So, I waited until Thursday. She didn't show.

Sweet Ashley was coming home from her mission within the next month and I thought it would be nice to invite her to attend our sacrament meeting (the facility lets residents attend our chapel for sacrament meeting on Sundays) and that might be easier to accommodate her situation. I called the facility again and they apologized about the "no show" on Thursday. I then told them about Ashley's homecoming and to invite this resident, we will call Lisa, to the meeting. "Um, I don't think she will be coming." "Oh, why not?" "Um, just a minute."

CHAPTER ELEVEN: YOU WILL BE FOUND!

There was a long pause and the young worker on the other end of the phone seemed to be a bit hesitant. Then she told me, "Well, Lisa is no longer here. We don't know where she is." What? You lost a patient? I couldn't believe my ears. The reality is, she bolted, and they could not force her to stay as it was an at will facility. She was wandering the area, and no one knew if she was in trouble, hurt, scared, or all of the above.

I panicked a little and did the first thing that came to my mind. I got on Facebook. Now, now, I know that doesn't sound wise, but for this instance, it led to a miracle. I looked up Ashley's friend contacts from her mission Facebook page and I found her! I took a risk and messaged her via Facebook, "Hi Lisa! It's Sister Porcelli's mom. How are you? We have been so worried about you. Are you still here in Utah or back in Toronto?"

I kid you not, but within five minutes I received a Facebook message back that she was waiting at a bus stop, about a mile from my home, ready to hop on board and ride to Salt Lake City. She wanted to catch a train from there and then head back to home. However, she had nothing with her but her phone. She had "run away" the night before in a panicked state of mind and forgot everything at the facility. I asked her to look up and find a street sign and tell me what it says so we could figure out where she was. When she read the words from the sign, we discovered she was standing right in front of my cousin's house and I told her, "Don't move. Don't get on that bus. We are coming to get you. We will help you with what you need."

I didn't know what the offered "help" would look like, but when I told Dean we needed to drop everything and go, he first looked at me like, "Gheez, crazy woman!" But I think he was then touched by the Spirit and we both hopped into action. We drove just a few minutes away and saw her standing there beneath the bus sign, shaking and a bit disheveled.

I jumped out of the car, ran to her, and gave her a big bear hug. We had never met each other before, but the Spirit was strong and our hearts connected. She wasn't afraid of us nor were we of her. It was as if we had known each other forever.

We then invited her to get into our car. She took a step or two forward but then hesitated as if there was more to tell us before we left. Then, everything seemed to be in slow motion. You know, those moments you can't quite make sense of, but know they are important? That pause was the Spirit working on all of us. She said, "I need to tell you a little bit more before we head to Salt Lake City." "That's fine, Lisa. Whatever it is, we are here to help you, not judge you," I said as I put my arm around her. I wanted her to understand we could handle whatever trouble she was in. My actions and words that night were not truly mine, but that of the Spirit.

She said she trusted us because she knew the character of my daughter and consequently felt safe being with us. She no longer hesitated and got into our car.

Lisa then shared that she had been abusing alcohol and drugs and was in a treatment center because her husband told her she had to do this, or their marriage would be over. He was a recent convert and wanted their family to eventually be sealed in the temple for all eternity. This meant Lisa had some hard habits to overcome. However, she only lasted a few weeks in treatment, got frustrated, and was heading home, taking a chance on saving her marriage, or not.

She said she had actually left the facility the day before, without any belongings, but walked back that night and slept on their grass. Early that morning she snuck inside, grabbed her phone, and then ran again. She had wandered all day looking for a liquor store and couldn't find anything. "I walked to three different cities and couldn't find any beer," she exclaimed, completely puzzled. We chuckled when she told us this because most people are not used to Utah, especially northern Utah County. We are super conservative and many cities do not serve liquor because there just isn't a customer base for it. It was not a coincidence her treatment facility was in that exact location. There is no other place on earth where she could have all these things in common:

1. Finding Ashley's missionary picture at the church house.
2. Walking all around not one, not two, but three different towns where she couldn't buy alcohol, thus preventing her from getting drunk and breaking her two weeks sobriety.
3. Finally ending up at a random street corner that "just happened" to be right in front of my cousin's home.

CHAPTER ELEVEN: YOU WILL BE FOUND!

Because of these miracles, we were able to find her exact location and offer assistance of a physical and spiritual nature. I know God had His hand in her story. She was a lost sheep and He needed someone to be His hands to guide her to safety.

Three Miracles So Far, and Counting

She revealed she hadn't eaten since the prior morning and was now starving. We asked if we could take her to dinner and then we would drop her off at the train station. She thought that was a good idea. We went to the Joseph Smith Memorial building and ate at the Garden Restaurant overlooking Temple Square. We all chatted for hours like old friends who hadn't seen each other in years. I couldn't believe the instant friendship we shared. We laughed and cried. Lisa had been converted to the gospel many years prior, but had then slipped away and gotten back into old habits. She knew all the scriptures and could recite correct answers to doctrine but had a hard time keeping the Word of Wisdom. She admitted to being an addict.

Normally, I would have completely avoid a person like this. You know how we are taught, "avoid the very appearance of evil," and other advice. However, I knew she wasn't evil. She was my sister in Christ, and I felt a strong connection to her. I knew we couldn't force her to stay in treatment and all we could do now is love her and make sure she was safe physically and mentally.

After dinner we purposefully drove around until just before her train was going to leave. Driving around a larger city at night, near a train station, makes for some interesting sightings. I was beginning to feel uneasy. Lisa was in the back seat of the car with Dean and myself up front. We heard sirens flying by as we passed people who were walking on the street. Some were clearly high on drugs and could barely make it down the dark alleys as they stumbled along the path. When we reached the train station, I assessed the sketchy behavior and witnessed people hanging around to see who they could sell drugs to or who to buy drugs from.

"Lisa, you don't belong here," I exclaimed.

"It's okay. I'm used to it. These are my people," she responded.

"Lisa, these are not your people anymore!" I replied, not realizing how offensive that could sound to someone. She looked confused and glared at me. I knew she was thinking, "How dare you judge them." But I stood firm. "Lisa, you can predict the future by past behavior. You already told us you walked miles to find a liquor store. Here, you will have easy access to anything you want. This is a pivotal moment. You say you want to save your marriage? Well, you must save yourself first!"

Okay, let's step back a minute. I know you may be thinking I am such a Karen. However, I believe there are times to be tolerant and there are times to be bold. When something is damaging to our bodies, minds, and souls, it's time to be bold. No more being complacent just so you won't offend someone. I took a risk at ruining this relationship and waited to hear her rebuttal.

No rebuttal came. "You're right," she said. I looked at Dean and asked her if she would like a priesthood blessing. "I would really love one," she said, looking a bit relieved at the offer. Dean looked at me confused as to "where" he could provide such a blessing, and drove around trying to find a spot that would be private enough. The only place we could pull over to have a little room was a dirt spot right across from the station. I wanted to argue with him about how dumb it was to pull into that exact spot, but he had already stopped the car, looking rather confident.

I then noticed there was not a streetlight there so at least attention wouldn't be directly upon us. Lisa looked at me, trying not to laugh, as the thought of receiving a priesthood blessing, all while drug exchanges were happening all around us, amused her. I then realized the reality of the situation and looked at Lisa and we both shrugged our shoulders and giggled under our breath. It definitely lightened the mood, and our spirits were lifted a bit.

She got into the front seat of our car, Dean stood just outside her door and placed his hands on her head. I stood watch next to him trying to offer some privacy. He gave Lisa a priesthood blessing of strength and comfort. He told her that angels were protecting her and that she could withstand temptation. He also endowed upon her that she would know what to say and do to save her marriage. We were all trying not to cry as it really was a beautiful experience, and we suddenly didn't care if others saw and witnessed the blessing.

CHAPTER ELEVEN: YOU WILL BE FOUND!

Once the prayer was over, we all hugged. I then looked inside the glass building and pointed to an older man with a long white beard. "See that man sitting on the end?" I asked Lisa.

"Yes."

"You are going to sit next to him and not move until the train comes. Don't talk to anyone and don't look at anyone. Your goal now is to take care of yourself, be safe, and don't be afraid to call upon Heavenly Father to protect you."

"I've got this," she said confidently.

Then, she was off and out of our care. I felt like a mother who just said goodbye to their kindergartener on the first day of school. My heart ached a little. I knew I had to trust the power of the priesthood and trust that Heavenly Father would take care of her. Although we couldn't control her personal decisions, she knew we believed in her. We were confident that she could be amongst the world without partaking of the world.

The In-Between— Letting Go of the Self

THE EXPERIENCE WITH LISA REMINDS ME OF HOW HARD IT CAN BE to find ourselves, and ultimately forgiving our own bad choices. I'm not talking about Lisa, but rather someone else, meaning myself. My story actually begins many decades prior. I remember being a young girl who was constantly doubted by society. I was hyperactive and always told to calm down. I felt like I was born to change the world, but others questioned my intentions, for I was but a silly girl. Their doubt began to seep into my soul, and I began to doubt myself. My once lofty goals were put aside while I took time to go to college, raise a family, and serve in whatever church calling I was asked to do. I was taught that women are to be feminine, quiet, and demure. I didn't have any of those qualities so I worked hard to fit into the lifestyle so many deem as "successful." I practiced sitting still and listening. I practiced styling my hair a certain way and wearing trendy clothes. I practiced how to talk and sound. After enough time, I began to fit in. I then began to blend in. I eventually couldn't find myself as everyone else looked and acted just like me. I was lost.

I had lost the vision of my dream I had when I was younger. But, I still wanted to save the world. I knew I was meant to be something more than the drone I was beginning to feel like. Because of my desire, Heavenly Father gave me many hardships and unique experiences so that I could someday find myself again. I started to realize I could be whomever I wanted to be. I learned I wasn't born to fit in, but to instead standout. People were put along my path, lessons were learned, and my confidence grew.

I view my past almost like an old movie, "This girl who had been abused as a teen, by an ex-boyfriend, found a kind man to marry, raised five wonderful children and then eventually earned a master's degree in counseling." The college classes were meant to prepare me for an occupation, but the reality is they were therapy for my soul. Heavenly Father's goal was not for me to earn a certificate, but the goal was to learn from the journey.

The experiences I have had have been manna to my spirit. I am blessed. I know this. When I learned about Lisa's situation, I knew all my experiences had led me to this moment of truth. Would I act on my impressions of the Spirit or ignore them, worried I was overstepping my bounds? I know the confidence I have gained over the years prepared me to be ready to serve someone I normally would have avoided. I did not fear.

One prophet that is an example of what can happen when we take the focus off of ourselves is Enos. He prayed for other souls, even praying for his enemies. What other miracles could be in store for us is we could be like Enos and pray for those we don't even know? That day with Lisa was a day I witnessed what can happen when we let God make the decisions. I can't explain it other than that.

Enos and Self-Forgiveness

We learn from Enos that, once we repent and humble ourselves, we will want to share the blessings of Christ's Atonement with others; "And there came a voice unto me, saying: Enos, thy sins are forgiven thee, and thou shalt be blessed. . . . Now, it came to pass that when I had heard these words I began to feel a desire for the welfare of my

CHAPTER ELEVEN: YOU WILL BE FOUND!

brethren, the Nephites; wherefore, I did pour out my whole soul unto God for them" (Enos 1:5, 9).

Enos was a good man, but he still felt he could do better. One day he was hunting in the forest for food, and he began to consider in his heart the words his father, who was the prophet at the time, had been sharing about Jesus Christ and eternal life.

Enos humbled himself and asked for forgiveness. God said that because Enos had faith in Jesus, his sins were forgiven. Enos was happy. But he didn't stop praying. He prayed for his friends and his enemies, the Nephites and the Lamanites. The Lord said he would bless them if they followed His commandments. Enos saw many wars between them but continued to be faithful and preach to them. He wanted to preserve the records his father Jacob had given him. The Lord promised him that someday He would give those records to the Lamanites.

One verse that stands out to me is verse 2: "And I will tell you of the wrestle which I had before God, before I received a remission of sins." Wow! I love the word "wrestle." If you have ever seen a wrestling match, you may witness twists and turns and the struggle to never give up. Enos was struggling with his own repentance. How often do we know we need to repent, but we fight it? I know I fight it. I have a lot of excuses of being too busy, too tired, too overwhelmed, or too anything to avoid the discomfort of the process.

However, through repentance we get more than just forgiveness. Not only are our hearts healed, but we receive a clearer vision of how to spend our time, talents, and efforts. Our entire being gets energized because we are allowing Heavenly Father to once again guide our minds and actions. Forgiving others then becomes easier and we are less likely to hold grudges toward others.

Repentance doesn't just free us from sin, but it can also free us from ill feelings towards leaders, neighbors, family members, and even strangers. When we feel good about ourselves, it is easier to feel good about others. Wounded relationships may heal because we create a space for them to heal. We become less judgmental and affected by those who aren't living the gospel principles. Instead of hating these so-called sinners, we begin to extend hands of friendship to them.

Different, Yet as One

Christ is an example of how we should treat those often labeled by others as "unworthy" or stereotyped as people to avoid. Christ, a Jew, approached a Samaritan woman and asks for a drink from a well. The woman was surprised, for Jews refuse to have anything to do with Samaritans. "Then said the woman of Samaria unto him, How is it that thou, being a Jew, askest drink of me, which am a woman of Samaria? For the Jews have no dealings with Samaritans" (John 4:9.) Jesus then told her that if she knew the gift God has for her, and who she was speaking to, she would ask Him, and He would give her what He calls Living Water.

She wondered about the well water already there and how it is different from Living Water. Jesus told her anyone who drinks the well water will soon become thirsty again. He then said, "But whosoever drinketh of the water that I shall give him shall never thirst; but the water that I shall give him shall be in him a well of water springing up into everlasting life" (John 4:14). The woman then pleads to be given the water, to never be thirsty again.

The women understands if she drinks water from the well, her physical thirst will only later return. But if she "consistently drinks" the word of God, known as the "living water," she will never spiritually thirst again. God continually offers up love and guidance. It is up to us to trust in Him and partake of His offer.

It can become common in the gospel to avoid others labeled as "not worthy" or stop interacting with those living contrary to gospel teachings. However, Christ is an example of how to reach out to others, meaning everyone, and share His light. We may be "different" from each other, yet we can become as one in purpose and example of the compassionate Christ.

CHAPTER ELEVEN: YOU WILL BE FOUND!

What This Means to Us

This resembles our willingness to stop relying on man to tell us what to do, what to wear, how to live, etc. but instead rely on Christ. Man's trends change. Technology changes. Relationships change. Careers change. Homes or environments change. However, Christ is constant. We will not be lost in the darkness if we repent, ask for forgiveness, and follow Him, always.

The Living Waters

Lisa had a decision to make that day we met one summer so long ago. She could have ignored me and gone her own way. She could have sternly told me to leave her alone and stay out of her business. She could have chosen to tell me exactly what I wanted to hear and then secretly done her own thing anyway. She could have just gone through the motions, pretending to accept our offer of help, then easily go back to her old ways once she made it home to Toronto. She could constantly pretend to have a testimony of the gospel yet fake her way through life. Her story has a miraculous ending because Lisa didn't choose any of those scenarios, but instead chose to follow Christ. She knew that not only the words that were said, but the priesthood blessing that was given and the feelings and hugs we shared, were not inspired by man, but of God.

Lisa reminds me of a modern day "Woman at the Well." I am so glad we didn't turn a blind eye to her out of our own fear or self-righteous judgement. The Spirit truly took over and guided our actions and words that day. Lisa was protected from drinking from "man's well," and thus surrender yet again to her addiction. Instead, she chose to drink of the Living Waters, leaning on the Lord. She decided to trust people she only knew as "Sister Porcelli's parents" because she knew the character of this special missionary. She determined to live up to her baptismal covenants and "thirst no more." She chose to be led by her Lord and Savior, her Living Waters.

So, What Happened?

Lisa went home to her family and, although she was worried they would reject her, they instead accepted her just as the father accepted the prodigal son—with open arms. She and her husband decided to work on their marriage by first living gospel principles. She called upon the Relief Society sisters to give her support. She sent me a picture a few weeks later of my missionary daughter sitting on a couch in her home.

Unbeknownst to her, my daughter had been upset she was "emergency transferred" the last few weeks of her mission. She was confused and didn't want to return to her prior area. There was a companionship that needed assistance, or so we thought.

When Ashley ran into Lisa in that same area, we all knew the real reason for the emergency transfer. It was God's intervention. We all knew the transfer was for her and Lisa to reunite in the gospel during a crucial time for both of them. There are no accidents.

God Knows You and Answers Prayers Individually

Over time Lisa became healthy in body and mind. A few years later she was called to teach the gospel doctrine class for Sunday School. I will never forget when we received an invitation to come and join her while she took out her temple endowments for the very first time. This happened in the middle of the pandemic and Lisa could only invite a certain number of people to be in the room with her. I hadn't been able to attend the temple in nearly a year's time. No one had. However, a few temples had opened for limited ordinances. She thought that day was a blessing for her, but it was a gift to all of us that were able to attend and witness with her, the power of God working on our souls. She grinned from ear to ear the entire ceremony. She has earned every blessing and is a true example of repentance, forgiveness, light, and love in the gospel of Jesus Christ.

God is mindful of Lisa, and He is mindful of you. He meets us where we are, not where others think we need to be. He knows you and answers prayers individually. Our job is to be open to the Spirit and willing to be led to higher ground. He knows each of us

CHAPTER ELEVEN: YOU WILL BE FOUND!

individually. He hears our prayers and connects to our hearts. He is mindful of your needs. He cries when you cry. He laughs when you laugh. He loves you. He needs you to be part of His kingdom. He may not make life easy, but it shouldn't be easy. We can witness miracles in our lives every day and recognize the times Heavenly Father has reached out to us, put light on our paths, forgiven our sins, and helped us along the way.

From working with kids in school, getting skinned knees from falling bikes, to chasing my papa's airplanes, I have learned God is in the details. It is up to us to listen, feel, and look to His light.

I am honored to share these insights and stories with you. I am grateful to those in my life who have been willing to support my journey. My heart is full of love for you! Now, let's get on with the business of living a life full of faith, devotion, and joy. May you know Heavenly Father as individually as He knows you. Look up. Don't hesitate in the gospel. You will be found.

. . . .

About the Author

....

Michelle is an entrepreneur, counselor, TEDx Speaker, and Play Therapist. She is a writer and instructor for BYU HS Independent Study and has spoken at Education Week and Especially For Youth.

Michelle lives in the Rocky Mountains with her patient husband, two exceptionally perfect grandchildren, five wonderful children, one beautiful daughter-in law, three French Bulldogs, and one attack cat named Robert.

Before she started writing Latter-day Saint non-fiction, Michelle earned a bachelor's degree from Brigham Young University. After that, just to shake things up, she went to graduate school and received a Master of School Counseling degree. She currently works as an elementary school counselor, where she feels like Mrs. Clause every day.

She loves chocolate chip cookies and homemade bread.

Her Motto: "Chins Up, Smiles On!"

Scan the QR Code to Visit

http://www.michelleporcelli.com/

You've dreamed of accomplishing your publishing goal for ages—holding *that* book in your hands. We want to partner with you in bringing this dream to light.

Whether you're an aspiring author looking to publish your first book or a seasoned author who's been published before, we want to hear from you. Please submit your manuscript to:

CEDARFORT.SUBMITTABLE.COM/SUBMIT

CEDAR FORT IS CURRENTLY PUBLISHING BOOKS IN THE FOLLOWING GENRES:

- LDS Nonfiction
- Cookbooks
- Biographies
- General Nonfiction
- Children's
- Self-Help
- Comic & Activity books
- Children's books with customizable characters